PICKLED PASSENGERS

The Story of the Sentinel-Cammell Na[...] Railcars

This is the story of some of the most extrao[...] on to the narrow-gauge tracks of the world. Imagine a coach [...] ntrols inside with the passengers. What would that be like? H[...]

As we shall see, the Sentinel rail cars were u[...] and on railways of very different character. But much of the history [...] is uncertain: there is little or no information about some of the cars, and the [...] that there is can be both unclear and contradictory. Even the works list is a very dubious friend. According to that most reliable of sources, the Records Officer of the Sentinel Drivers' Club, Anthony R. Thomas, most Sentinel records were destroyed when the remains of the company were taken over by Rolls Royce.

When Rolls Royce took over the Sentinel in 1975 the first thing they did was to destroy all records of steam vehicles, probably to stop enthusiasts like you and me constantly pestering them. Some employees were disgusted and 'rescued' some items from the skip before it was burned.

Maybe we can produce a second edition of this volume when people from all around the world have written in to point out the many mistakes or to add facts which are at present undiscovered. Meanwhile, I am indebted to those who have gone out of their way to provide text and photographs; their names are given later and if I have missed someone, please forgive me. The mistakes are all mine.

Although it is well-known that the Sentinel Company built geared locomotives of many gauges, perhaps their greatest fame in railway circles is reserved for the splendid rail cars which they built for the LNER and LMS, amongst others. These had wonderful names like *Tally-ho*, taken from the names of stage-coaches which, if you are of a fanciful turn of mind, you might suppose they replaced. Many of these machines went overseas, and the design reached its peak in the three-car unit, Sentinel 5208 of the Egyptian Railways, with a diesel-fired boiler, which is preserved at Quainton Road.

Although our interest here is in narrow-gauge cars (less than "standard" or 4ft 8½in), there is a sense in which the division between standard- and narrow-gauge is false. The British standard loading gauge is very restricted whilst many narrow-gauge loading gauges are generous. The early narrow-gauge Sentinels for the Jersey Railway (3ft 6in gauge) are shown on drawings as being 8ft 6in wide whilst the first (standard-gauge) car for the LNER was only 8ft! Later LNER cars were 9ft wide. Generally the rail cars are shown in drawings or tables of dimensions as between 8ft 6in and 9ft 4in wide and in at least one case the bodies supplied for narrow- and standard-gauge cars for the same customer were identical.

Before we look at these rail cars, let us remind ourselves of the background against which they were built.

The firm of Alley and MacLellan, formed in Glasgow in 1875, was known from the beginning for the excellence of its engineering. At first they made valves and other fittings: they gave their products the name *Sentinel*. Soon they were manufacturing marine steam engines and stationary

The first Super-Sentinel wagon in Glasgow, belonging to the Sighthill contractor Archibald Alexander.
Photograph: Glasgow City Council, Glasgow Museums

engines; they made steam-assisted steering-gear for ships and it seems that they were extremely competitive, perhaps because they organised their factory in Polmadie Road, Glasgow along very efficient lines so that each operation was carried out in ideal conditions and then the production line moved the item on.

In 1903, Alley and MacLellan took over the firm of Simpson and Bibby of Horsehay, Shropshire who had been designing and producing steam road waggons (note the double g); their work was transferred to Polmadie. Along with Daniel Simpson and George Woodvine from that company, Stephen Alley, son of the founder, went on to design, patent and build waggons in great numbers. It need not concern us here how those waggons developed from the "Standard" beginnings to the "Super" waggons, suffice to say that, until road regulations were changed in 1930, when steam vehicles became subject to almost impossible conditions, the business boomed. Between 1906 and 1929, over eight thousand were built.

The basic Sentinel design, whether for road or rail operations, involved a patented vertical boiler and steam plant which turned the wheels, at first by means of chains, and later through a geared drive, thus providing plenty of power from a relatively small and economical engine. Stories abound of prodigious runs completed whilst consuming only moderate amounts of fuel. This and Alley's reputation for superb engineering ensured that Sentinels outshone their rivals.

Kyrle W. Willans worked with Alley to produce a geared railway locomotive, the first of which was outshopped in 1923 (Sentinel works number 5156) a month after the first rail car. Although we are not going to spend much time on locomotives in this study, it is interesting to note that this, too, was a narrow-gauge machine. It was built for the 2ft 5½in gauge. Sentinel locomotives went on to make a significant contribution to the rail industry, and some are preserved. For a narrow-gauge example, refer to the Narrow Gauge Railway Museum's *Nutty*, which is a well-travelled machine.

In 1922 Sentinel produced a catalogue entitled *Sentinel Steam Rail Coaches* in which the most enthusiastic language outlined the advantages of using the eponymous vehicles, this despite the fact that none had yet been produced! A single extract will give the flavour of the thing; the as yet unbuilt coach is compared to a Sentinel road vehicle:

On railway work there is no steering to be done and no comparable grades to negotiate, so that the driving reduces itself to a little stoking (about 4lbs of coal per mile), watching the water level in the boiler gauge glass, and in using the throttle and brakes as required. The result is that a reasonably intelligent man, European or native, can be safely trusted to drive a "Sentinel" Rail Coach with a minimum of training.

More about the various catalogues that survive may be found in Appendix 1.

The works list in *Abbott* (see below) shows that over seventy narrow-gauge rail cars were built between 1923 and 1937 and two more in 1953. Other than the Jersey cars, none was built for railways in the British Isles. For a note on the works list and its source in Abbott, please see the bibliography at the end of this book.

When the first cars were constructed, they used bodywork made by Cammell Laird & Co, although Cammell Laird became a part of Metropolitan-Cammell Carriage, Wagon & Finance Co. Ltd ('Metropolitan-Cammell', later MetroCammell) in 1929. How this cooperation between the two firms began is uncertain, though in 1923, Cammells were a leading manufacturer of railway equipment and so would be a good choice of partner for a firm which must have known next to nothing about railways. Later, relationships between the two concerns were not always totally harmonious, however (see Appendix 2).

The rail cars that were produced fall into two main groups. From 1923 until 1927 they had vertical boilers, two double-acting cylinders and a chain drive to the wheels. These cars were articulated, with a tractor unit and trailer coach. In this way, the chain could be easily run from engine to wheels. From 1928 a new, six cylinder, single acting engine was used. This drove the wheels by means of a gearbox and cardan shaft, so allowing the cars to be rigid. More details of the mechanical arrangements are given in Appendix 3.

The various designs may conveniently be broken into six types:

1. The first batch: 1923-5

These "pioneer" cars (the first two were actually named *The Pioneer, Nos 1 & 2*) were really straight adaptations of Super-Sentinel road vehicles. They had the usual Sentinel coal-fired vertical boiler (though Abbott notes, probably wrongly, that the very first had a horizontal boiler!) which supplied steam at 230 lbs per square inch to the two double-acting horizontal cylinders of 6¾ x 9in. These used the Sentinel poppet-valve system and drove the 2ft 6inch diameter wheels through a chain-drive. On the first car there was just one chain, but subsequent vehicles had separate chains driving each pair of wheels. It seems likely that there was a 2:1 reduction in the drive chain. As outlined above, because of the need to keep the chain in alignment with the wheels, the cars were articulated so that the driving end carried the passenger carriage in a kind of piggy-back arrangement, with a leather weather-proof connection at the sides and a steel plate roof between the two. This driving portion also contained the coal bunker (often provided with a roof mounted hopper) and the water tank. A system of levers allowed most cars to be driven from the rear, or No. 2 end.

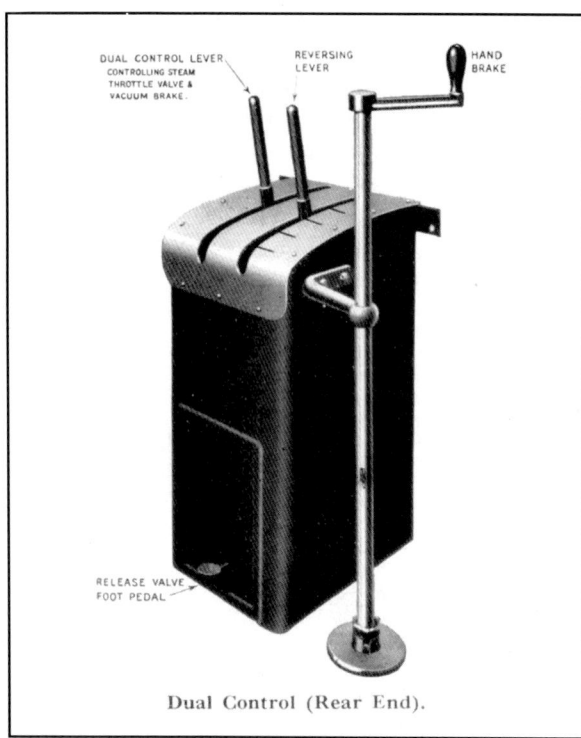

There were ten of this type of narrow-gauge car built.

Top: dual control (rear end) -1925 catalogue. Above: Sentinel-Cammell railcar The Pioneer *waiting at the extension platform at St. Aubin, Jersey c.1930s. (Jim Lake collection)*

2. The "vertical" cars: 1926-7
Records of this type of car are difficult to come by, but it seems certain that they were very similar to their predecessors. The boilers, articulation and chain-drive were almost certainly all retained, though working pressure seems to have been raised to 275 psi. The cylinders (still two double-acting 6¾ x 9inch) were arranged vertically, a system which would have taken up less space in the driving part of the vehicle and is said to have allowed a better poppet-valve layout. Fourteen of these cars were built for narrow-gauge railways, and for the first time there were some two-car units which seem to have had the "works" in the middle with the two cars piggybacked as before (see the section for the Bengal-Nagpur Railway).

3. 100 – 150 hp Single Rail Car with a vertical boiler.
Built from 1928 onwards, these cars were given single-acting six-cylinder engines which lay horizontally under the frames, driving the nearest bogie via a gearbox and a cardan shaft. Because of this new configuration, articulation between the driving compartment and coach was no longer necessary and the cars were built rigid. Most, if not all, had a driving cab at the No. 2 end.

A two-car Sentinel rail car on the Federated Malay States Railway. (©2008 Hakcipta Tak Terpelihara Brader DM)

4. 100 – 150 hp Articulated Rail Car with a vertical boiler.
In most respects these cars were similar to the single cars noted at 3. above, but a central bogie supported a second coach which was provided with a driving cab at the outer end, making these a steam forerunner of two-car diesel multiple units.

5. 200 – 300 hp Single Rail Car with a horizontal, Woolnough Boiler.
The larger boiler in these cars allowed the provision of two of the six-cylinder single acting engines, making the cars suitable for heavier, more steeply graded work.

6. 200 – 300 hp Articulated Rail Car with a horizontal, Woolnough Boiler
These were a two-car version of the cars noted at 5. above. One engine drove the "front" bogie and one the bogie which provided articulation with the second coach.

There were fifty-four six cylinder cars of types 3 - 6 built from 1928 to 1953.

In recognition that some railways had difficulty finding suitable coal, and that coal was a difficult fuel to use at high altitudes, an oil-fired option was available with a different boiler. As the cars developed some had boilers placed in the centre section of the coach, thus ensuring that the passengers got the maximum effect of the heat produced. This seems to have been particularly popular in oil-fired cars.

All the rail cars had 2ft 6inch driving wheels, apart, possibly, from a few Indian cars.

All these versions needed a driver, a fireman and a guard for operation, though undoubtedly some railways tried to reduce the staff to two to reduce costs, particularly on oil-fired cars.

In the catalogue, Sentinel claimed that the cars were exported fully fitted inside but in primer or undercoat on the exterior. At least one railway claims to have fitted out its own cars, however. Generally, the cars (which were, of course built by Metropolitan-Cammell) seem to have had similar interiors, so the catalogue claim seems reasonable. Often reversible, tram-style, seats were fitted: those in New Zealand were padded leather, but the Palestinian ones were slatted wood.

There seem to have been two basic types of seating used, either the slatted wooden affairs, or upholstered. First, there were longitudinal bench seats as shown in the photos of the Sri Lankan cars. This arrangement was able to accommodate large numbers of passengers, although many of them would have had to stand. The pictures of 331 in Sri Lanka show London Transport style straps above the line of seats.

The second type of seating was transverse; some was what we might call tram-style, where the seat back could be reversed according to the direction of travel. We are fortunate that the picture of New Zealand's Rm-1 shows this (see picture on page 18).

Other cars had more traditional fixed seating, especially in first class. The picture on page 9 of SP4 (Tasmanian Government Railway) is a good example.

Never forget that these cars were built by Metropolitan-Cammell; at the time that our Sentinels were being built, that firm was engaged, amongst other work, on building stock for the London

Interior of Ceylon Government Railways 331. (James Waite)

Interior of SP4 (Stuart Dix)

Underground. A quick glance at the interior pictures we have might almost persuade us that we are on the District Line!

In *The Hedjaz Railway* by R. Tourret, we learn of the Palestine cars:

The window openings in all compartments were provided with raising lights and louvres, all framed in teak. The sliding side doors were carried on 'Critall' runner gear. 'Monarch' roof ventilators were fitted in all passenger and luggage compartments. The lighting installation was the Pyle National type with 1500 watt turbo-generator at the rear of the engine cab. Lighting was provided in all passenger and luggage compartments. The cars were also provided with a headlight mounted at each end of the car, together with tail and indicator lights. Electric signal bells were fitted in each driver's compartment with a push-button operating each at the opposite end of the car. A steam whistle was mounted on the cab roof at the leading end of the car operated from both driver's compartments.

Much of this must have applied to all cars.

Usually, latterly always, there was a driver's compartment at both ends of the car or cars, that at the rear having control rods carried along the underframes. These controls were said to be positive and easily manipulated with removable handles to prevent unauthorised use. Usually a vacuum brake was provided. Sanding gear could be arranged for and cowcatchers were often fitted to exported cars.

The rear-end driver's cab of a (later) car (1932 catalogue)

Extracts from the 1932 Sentinel catalogue explaining much of the engine and boiler arrangements in more detail are to be found in Appendix 1.

The Sentinel catalogues make extravagant claims about the performance of their vehicles. The style of the catalogues may be judged from the following statements made in the 1932 edition:

Now we are going to be frank. When we sell you a locomotive we make what we consider the fair manufacturing profit of 10 per cent. nett, or £120. When you buy a locomotive from us it can save you at least 100 per cent. per annum on its first cost for many years, and you benefit much more by the transaction than we do. Why not, therefore, write us to-day?

Claims for top speed and performance seem, in the light of facts we shall see later, rather exaggerated:

These cars, which cost about £4000 each, can haul under suitable conditions and at a very low cost per mile, a trailer car, goods truck or horsebox and are provided with buffers and couplings for that purpose. Their speed reaches 60 miles an hour under favourable conditions and, when suitably geared for hauling a trailer, the maximum speed is limited by the safe maximum revolutions of the engine to about 45 miles an hour.

A generally very optimistic view is taken of all aspects of the business. Today, the Trade Descriptions Act might come into play.

The first orders received from an English railway delivered a little over three months ago were for two coaches. They went straight into service, and both have now run 20,000 miles to the satisfaction of their owners. We believe these coaches make nearly all their own traffic for they run special services, and estimate from data taken during their running that each of them nets surplus earnings at the rate of over £5000 a year after meeting all running costs and amortisation. They should each have a life of at least 20 years and during each of these years will probably earn a surplus considerably greater than their entire first cost. They fully come up to our guarantees, and when, as we hope, more are ordered, these will put up still better performances.

And so on. In fact, very few rail cars lasted in full service for twenty years, although the standard of engineering does seem to have been very good, and there are some cars still in existence today. Nowhere, however, is a Sentinel rail car still in service with its steam plant intact (though one such does still exist). The advent of efficient diesel engines, as with the road lorries, put paid to the steam cars. After all, diesel vehicles require fewer staff, they run without long preparation and they do not generally introduce a tropical atmosphere into the passenger accommodation.

There is little doubt that the success of the Jersey cars and of the standard-gauge, mostly LNER cars, induced many railways to bow to the persuasive language of the catalogue. That many of these overseas railways had track far inferior to the British permanent way may explain why success was not always assured. There is good primary evidence of the running of the narrow-gauge cars in only a few cases; these are reported below. In some cases, there is anecdotal evidence, or suggestive facts available which have encouraged me to imagine what riding in the vehicles may have been like; again, this is given below, but with a clear statement that it is conjectural. The history of these cars is rapidly fading into the past, so we must do our best to record it whilst we can. May I encourage anyone who sees inaccuracies in this account, or who can add to it, to make contact?

THE CARS AND THEIR RAILWAYS

The cars are dealt with under the title of the railway which ordered them, and the railways are listed in the order that they became customers of Sentinel. Publications mentioned are listed in the Bibliography.

Jersey

The Sentinel railmotor story began, not with those well-known standard-gauge examples, but with a car built to the 3ft 6in gauge of the Jersey Railway. Fittingly, this wonderful machine was named *The Pioneer*; it was Sentinel works number 4863 and was rather a leap of faith on the part of the railway authorities. It is true that steam railmotors of other makes were working on other lines, but nothing quite like this had been seen before. We must assume that the reputation which Sentinels had gained with their road vehicles stood them in good stead with the directors in Jersey.

The Jersey Railway ran for nearly eight miles from St Aubin to Corbière. Built to standard gauge it was converted to 3ft 6in gauge and lengthened in 1884. It was, of course, originally locomotive worked and the narrow-gauge locos which worked the completed line were four in number: two were Manning Wardles and two Bagnalls. They proved very expensive to run and, particularly when bus services were introduced in the island, they were economic suicide for the company. The railcars were able to operate similar services using about a fifth of the amount of coal!

The Pioneer was an articulated car, 56ft 9in long over headstocks. It was, in fact, slightly longer than this overall as its ends were curved outwards. The power unit or tractor, contained in the front part which was about 12ft long, had a vertical boiler and two-cylinder engine. The boiler worked at a pressure of 230lb/ square inch and each cylinder had a diameter of 6¾in and a stroke of 9in. Transmission was via a single chain. This equipment was exactly the same as that fitted to Super-Sentinel road waggons, including the unorthodox poppet-valves. This front part was joined to the rest of the car by a flexible connection. The tractor wheelbase was 7ft 3in and the rear wheels projected beyond the back of the tractor unit so as to support the front of the trailer. Both parts were a steel body on wooden frames

In the trailing passenger portion (42ft 8in approx) there were originally 56 seats (Bonsor says 64 in *The Jersey Railway*) divided between twelve in the first class and 44 in second. First-class seats were royal blue plush and at least some were reversible tram-style seats, and the seconds were of bronze-coloured cloth. It is reported that there was a post box fitted, but the evidence is inconclusive about where that might have been. It seems that first-class passengers would have had a splendid view of the working portion, and, if later reports are to be believed, they were able to share in the heat and smoke as well.

When *The Pioneer* made its first run on 18 June 1923, it was seen to be both quiet and efficient. The three and three quarter mile journey from St. Helier to St. Aubin's was completed in twelve minutes, notwithstanding the fact that the machine reached 35 mph at one point. The rest of the journey must have been very slow! It seems that everyone expressed themselves satisfied with the runs made that day, despite the reported fact that on the last run the leading axle broke. This was quickly remedied and the car put into service, where considerable savings of coal and time were made.

Bonsor reports that in the forward direction (i.e. with the steam portion at the front) the railmotor required only a "driver-cum-fireman" but that when travelling the other way a guard needed to act

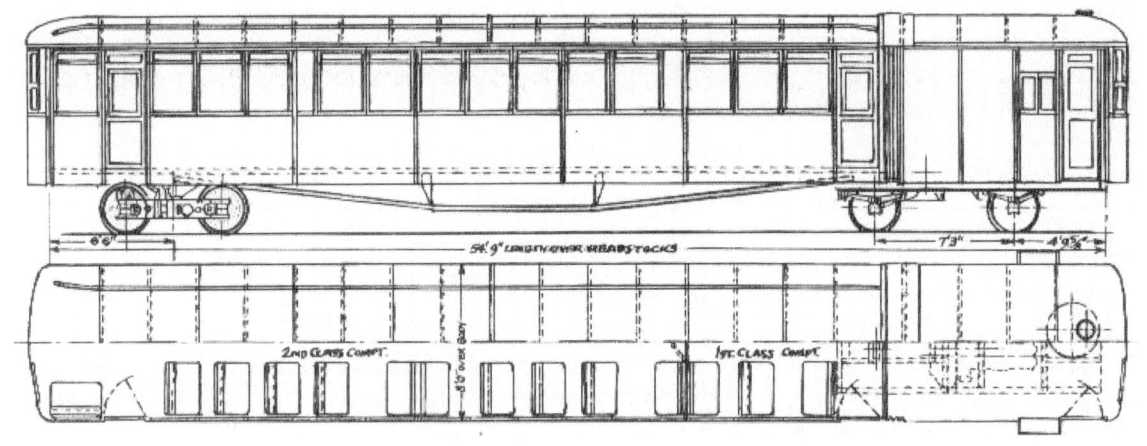

General arrangement drawing of The Pioneer. *Here, there is no rear driving facility shewn.*

as brakesman. Given that road Sentinels generally had a driver and mate at this stage, the mate acting as fireman, it seems more likely that three staff (driver, fireman, guard) were needed. Various sources, including an early plan drawing, suggest, too, that *The Pioneer, No. 1* could be driven only from the front, articulated end but that it was later changed to enable driving from the "back". Be that as it may, it could not be turned on Jersey and so saved considerable time at the ends of its journeys, as locomotive trains had to run round.

By 28 June all was in a suitable condition for a number of dignitaries to be entertained on the car. A senior Sentinel official, Mr G. Butler Lloyd, entertained potential foreign customers and congratulated the Jersey Railways and Tramways Limited on being the first concern to introduce the new railmotor. Since quite a number of the cars were subsequently sold abroad (no other narrow-gauge cars went to domestic customers) we must assume that all was satisfactory, or at least that Sentinels persuaded people that it was so.

It must be remembered that the railway on Jersey was a very short affair. The longest journey that could be undertaken was just over 7½ miles, and high speeds were neither desirable nor practicable. These considerations might explain why the Jersey cars were reckoned such a success whilst similar cars elsewhere (in Tasmania for example, see below) were intensely disliked for their rough riding, overbearing heat and smoke, and noise.

In Jersey another similar machine followed; less imaginatively than before it was named *The Pioneer No. 2* (Later it was renamed *Portelet* – Sentinel 5159 of January 1924). The quick delivery of the second machine suggests that it was already contemplated, if not ordered when *No. 1* arrived. *No. 2* was very like its predecessor, except that it was certainly capable of being driven from both ends, a fact which meant that there were four fewer second-class seats. It also had double chain drive, making it more reliable; the consequent gearing-down that this allowed meant that the car was better able to work the hilly part of the line to Corbière. Some sources say that it was delivered along with a trailer coach which had both luggage space and nineteen more seats. So far no picture of this trailer has been found, a picture in *Railways of the Channel Islands*, undoubtedly being of a different coach of much greater capacity.

Another publicity stunt followed the introduction of No. 2. This time representatives from Australia, France and the London Midland & Scottish Railway were present. An excellent description of this demonstration is given by Hughes and Thomas. Again, it must have been a success, for, as we shall see, railmotors were provided for all three of those present. Indeed, some were built in France under licence by Les Ateliers de Construction du Nord, although not until 1935 and then using Doble engines supplied by Sentinel.

A third railmotor, *La Moye* (Sentinel 5833), joined *Nos. 1 & 2*. This machine was often referred to as "the Wembley car" as it had been on display at the Wembley exhibition; it arrived on Jersey in 1925. If reports are to be believed these cars transformed the fortunes of the ailing railway, as mentioned previously, using a fifth of the coal that a locomotive would have used. When all three railmotors were working, no locomotive trains were needed.

A fourth, standard-gauge, car (Sentinel 5655), named *Normandy* (or *Normandie* – both forms are seen), had been provided in 1925 for the Jersey Eastern Railway, and when that concern closed, it was converted to the narrow gauge and joined its stable mates. A fifth car, *Brittany (Brittanie)* also worked on the standard gauge and it is interesting to note in passing that this car is the only one of the five to survive in any form; its passenger trailer, having been used as a garden shed and then taken into the care of the Pallot Steam Museum, is at the time of writing subject to a restoration programme. Its tractor unit went to SE England as an industrial loco and was presented to the Kent and East Sussex Railway in the 1960s where it was allegedly broken up, as no-one realised its historical value. Its engine is believed to have been re-used in the restoration of a Sentinel loco.

Brittanie: *the trailer in use as a garden shed at Greve d'Azette, Jersey in the 1970s. Although this car was of standard gauge, its picture is included here as it is the only known survivor of a trailer from an articulated car. It is likely that the narrow-gauge conversion of* Normandie *had a trailer of the same type. (Chris Totty)*

When delivered, *Nos. 1 & 2* were painted in a yellow livery with dark lines, but by 1931 the cars were reportedly in green and cream. Photographs confirm that *Normandy* was so painted, but so far no confirmation of that livery for the other cars is available. Most photographs of *Nos. 1 & 2* suggest that a darker livery was used in the late twenties. However, reports that the cars bore a maroon livery probably result from confusion with the livery of the Jersey Eastern Railway, although it is perfectly possible that *Normandy* ran in that livery after conversion.

The Pioneer, No. 1, seems to have been scrapped in 1935. Perhaps parts of it might still exist! Nothing could compensate, however, for a disastrous fire in 1936 which finished off the railway altogether. St. Aubin's station caught fire early on Sunday morning, 18 October and sixteen passenger coaches stored there were destroyed. The company, teetering on the edge of financial disaster, decided it could not continue. The remaining railcar tractors were used in the dismantling of the line and were then broken up. Very little of the railway or its railmotors survives, but what does remain is of enduring interest. The route of the railway is today a pleasant coastal path, along which the initiated can see evidence of stations. The St. Helier Tourist Information Office used to be in the erstwhile station building.

The railmotors were able to run four times an hour each (i.e. two return journeys) between St. Helier and St. Aubin's so that two cars could run a quarter-hourly service. More usually, during the summer season, a half-hour service seems to have been the rule. However, every fourth train or so was extended to run along the whole of the railway to Corbière, so it seems likely that three cars were used at peak times. Around St. Aubin's Bay, from St. Helier to St. Aubin's, the trackbed is nearly level, but on the extension to Corbière there is a 1 in 40 gradient to Don Bridge and 1 in 60 climb to the summit. There is then a 1 in 100 drop to Corbière. Passing places were provided on the single track at Millbrook and Don Bridge. From 1931, there was no winter service.

Orki Division, India

According to the best works list available, works numbers 5155 and 5158 were railcars, but Simon Darvill's excellent *Industrial Locomotives of South Asia* suggests that they were locomotives. Jacks of Karachi, now in Pakistan, obtained these two metre-gauge vehicles for their Orki Division works in Rajasthan (present-day India). Jacks were a company who carried out canal building and irrigation works in the Punjab region; they had a large fleet of locomotives and were agents for Sentinel in India. It is difficult to see why they would need railmotors and Simon Darvill suggests that they owned, inter alia, 2ft 6in gauge 4w Sentinel 7728 of 1929 (probably a loco), and 6713 of 1926 also a loco. Orki is in Rajasthan, on the rail line between Shivpur and Hindu Malkot, just over twenty kilometres from Shri Ganganagar. These two vehicles may have been railmotors, but, if so, no details of them have come to light.

Commonwealth Railways, Australia

During the early 1920s it was decided that an improvement to the passenger service on the North Australia Railway (NAR) was required. The main stimulus for this upgrade was the frequent need for the railway to provide special trains to take seriously ill or injured people to hospital or to transport the mail. As a result, in 1924 the first Sentinel-Cammell steam rail coach to operate in Australia was purchased for the NAR. A steam powered vehicle was chosen over an internal combustion engine, basically because a good complement of steam fitters was based in Darwin.

The NAR car, works no 5234 of July 1924 to 3ft 6in gauge, was similar in design to the Jersey cars (it was articulated and had two horizontal cylinders) although its bodywork differed slightly. The

Leaping Lena, on the North Australia Railway. Photo: Northern Territory Library

standard-gauge type of front end with three windows forward was fitted and the passenger saloon was provided with shades after initial journeys made that necessary. We must assume that the reports from Jersey emphasised the smooth running of the cars, as it was intended to transport injured people from outlying districts, but the reality turned out to be somewhat different. The car was soon nicknamed *Leaping Lena!* Because the car was expected to achieve higher speeds than locomotive hauled trains, the journey from Darwin to Katherine could, it was hoped, be made in one day, avoiding the overnight stop then taken. Darwin to Katherine is a distance of about 320 km., so considerable speeds were expected. In fact it seems that the Sentinel operated only from Katherine to Birdum (186 km.) and that only once a fortnight. For this journey, nearly six hours were allowed.

The injector could not maintain the necessary supply of water to the boiler over the distances the journey entailed. This seems to have been a recurring problem with Sentinels; even the LNER suffered in this way! Moreover, the inside of the unit was plagued by the presence of smoke and by excessive heat. An extended chimney was added, but nothing could change the motion.

It has been suggested (by Jim Harvey in *Australian Railway Historical Society Bulletin*) that the Sentinel was intended for British permanent way and the Australian equivalent was "low budget", but this magnanimity probably masks the truth. On Jersey the distance over which passengers had to endure was a matter of a few miles. Over a hundred or so miles the journey became a nightmare. Jim Harvey goes on: *...the guard had to write out the tickets before departure as it was impossible to write once the car was in motion. In fact it was impossible to read, to sleep or even sit still. Seats were so hard passengers preferred to lie on the floor. The guard had the best ride. He was able to make up a bed of sorts using mail bags and other suitable parcels or van goods... the average person could survive the journey only by taking liberal doses of strong stimulants.*

The railway management's first attempt to improve the lot of the passenger was to alter the pitch of the seats. Then in November 1931 the springs in the rear bogie were modified but with little effect. As a last resort the trailing bogie was replaced with one from a former South Australian 'Short Tom' carriage of a design dating back to the 1880s. This last modification was reported on 9 April 1934 but only two weeks later officials claimed that the riding left much to be desired. The Chief Mechanical

Engineer for Commonwealth Railways visited Darwin the following year and gave the opinion that further expenditure on the vehicle could not be justified.

When the new Commissioner made his first visit to the Top End in 1930 he was astonished to find that the car was operated by a staff of three; driver, fireman and guard. Was the fireman really necessary? Yes came the emphatic reply. The cabin was too hot and the unit too unreliable to be left to the driver alone.

Much of the data relating to the problems of the Sentinel car can be found in a letter written by the railways in reply to an enquiry from William Adams & Co. the Melbourne agents. Adams were told that the unit operated a more or less regular service between Katherine and Birdum once per fortnight during the 1930s, a round trip totalling 371 km. For the three year period ending 30 June 1934 the car ran a total of 20406 km at a cost of 12/5d km, bare operating costs excluding overheads. Materials consumed during the return run were listed: coal, 0.71 tonnes; water, 4273 lt; cylinder oil, 4.54 lt; grease, ½ kilogram; waste, ½ kilogram; and firewood 18 kilograms.

Eventually the car broke down and, after repair was involved in a crash when it was being hauled back to Katherine. It was considered unsuitable for further repair. It languished at the workshops at Darwin for some time. But in 1942 some American airmen, disgusted with the inability of the authorities to move their equipment inland, ripped out the steam unit and fitted an internal combustion engine to form a makeshift rail tractor. When the aforementioned authorities found out they banned its use! The trailer was, however, used in a petrol-hauled railcar from 1942 until 1955. It was later purchased for scrap by a Japanese salvage team. So ended one of the most unusual Sentinel stories.

1925 catalogue photo of the South African car

Griffin Engineering Co., South Africa

In August 1924 Sentinel works number 5245 was completed for the Griffin Engineering Company of Johannesburg, South Africa. Mechanically, this car was almost certainly the same as the Jersey cars and it was to the same 3ft 6in gauge.

Griffin Engineering was active in South Africa for a number of years and appears to have been instrumental in land clearances so that railway and other developments could be pushed forward without hindrance. It is impossible to find references to the company in modern South African publications.

New Zealand

Rm-1, supplied to NZ Railways in 1925 was, according to a later historian, found unsuitable for local conditions. The car measured 56½ft overall, and weighed a little under 20 tons in working order. Seating accommodation was provided for 48 passengers, and the body was of steel construction. The gauge was 3ft 6in.

As in Jersey, the power unit was articulated, and a vertical boiler mounted in the driving compartment supplied steam at a pressure of 270 lb./sq. in. to two cylinders 6¾in. diameter x 9in. stroke, the output being 75 hp at 450 rpm. Transmission from the crankshaft to the two driving axles was effected by chains and sprockets. The vehicle was designed for a maximum speed of 45 mph. Sufficient water was carried for 50 miles, and the bunker held enough coal for 80. Dual controls, vacuum brake, and electric lighting were installed.

A rare view! The interior of Rm-1, the New Zealand Car. 31 January 1925 Photograph: Albert Percy Godber, 1875-1949, courtesy: Alexander Turnbull Library, Wellington, New Zealand.

A works catalogue photo of the New Zealand Car: it appears to be unfinished.

After tests on the Hutt line the Sentinel-Cammell car was transferred in 1926 to Frankton where it was employed on a night passenger service to Thames. It is said that the railcar was inclined to be rough riding when partly laden. There were also mechanical shortcomings and the vehicle was withdrawn from service in 1927. Twenty years later a portion of the steel body could be seen lying in long grass in a paddock at Lower Hutt.

It seems that tests carried out on the Wellington-Melling line led to the conclusion that the car was not able to maintain the speeds required for suburban traffic. Its only use in revenue service seems to have been the above-mentioned night service on the Frankton-Thames line, a distance of about 63 miles. It left Frankton Junction as train 313 at 10.35pm and arrived at Thames at 2.15am, a running time of three hours and forty minutes, or an average speed of about 17 mph; however, there were twenty-four possible stops, some of which were made if requested. It was described in an official report as a "subsidised newspaper train". Its return journey began at 3.15am and it arrived back at Frankton at 6.30am in time to connect with an express to Auckland. After two years or so, a locomotive-hauled train was substituted.

Problems seem to have beset this car from all sides. The residents around the line at Thames complained that its whistle disturbed them during the night. This was the same whistle that drivers reported caused problems of loss of boiler pressure if used too much; and there were five level crossings near Frankton!

Because the car connected with main-line trains at Frankton, it fulfilled a useful purpose, and one report tells how that in December 1926, 59 people boarded at that station, with six more joining at Hamilton (six minutes out). With reportedly poor lighting, no heating and nearly a four-hour journey to endure, that must have been quite an experience.

The Thames branch was part of the railways of the North Island of New Zealand. Some of it still exists; it left the East Coast main trunk railway at Morrinsville but is now cut short as the Waitoa Industrial Line. It passes through fairly flat country to end on the coast at the town of Thames, where the old station is preserved. Thames was closed to all traffic in 1995.

In 1927, the New Zealand Railways Magazine reported that this service was "one of the most popular trains ever introduced by the Department", but this was an official publication. The same article reveals that, although the car had controls at both ends, the rear ones were not used "as it is possible to turn the vehicle on the turntables provided at Thames and Frankton respectively."

Rm-1 had been modified by the New Zealand Railways in that the wooden wheel centres had been replaced with steel in order to operate track circuits on the Wellington suburban lines where it was tested. Even the official publication admitted that this may have been the cause of the rather rough riding experienced when the car was not full. A driver, fireman and guard were employed when the car was in service on the Thames branch.

The Sentinel-Cammell people must have thought: "It's an island, the gauge is 3ft 6in and they need a handy vehicle – it's just like Jersey." How wrong can you be!

Newfoundland Government Railway, Canada

The Newfoundland Railway operated on the island of Newfoundland from 1898 to 1988. With a total track length of 906 miles (1,458 km), it was the longest 3ft 6in (1,067 mm) narrow gauge railway system in North America.

Robert Cuff writes "After the government took over the railway in 1923 an effort was made to serve the less-travelled lines using trolley-like "day coaches" on the Bay de Verde, Trepassey and Heart's Content lines. The Bay de Verde and Trepassey lines were closed in winter, and in 1931 were closed altogether. As Heart's Content was a winter port for the A.N.D. (Anglo-Newfoundland Development) Company that line continued sporadically until 1938." We may assume that the "day coaches" were Sentinel works Nos. 5641 and 5711 supplied to the railway in 1925. They were designated 'A' and 'B'. Three years later works Nos. 7314-6 were delivered; they became 'C', 'D', 'E'.

The first two vehicles were similar to the Jersey cars, being chain driven and articulated with two vertical cylinders. Little is known about these cars. The 1928 cars, however, were rigid vehicles with a single six-cylinder engine driving through a gearbox and shaft. They were of the type designated by Sentinel as 100 – 150 hp and, according to the 1929 catalogue, the passenger saloons carried 15 first- and 29 second-class passengers, both sections having a lavatory. Almost half of the length of the car, however, was given over to luggage and mail compartments, each with a sliding door. These compartments separated the passengers from the boiler, no doubt improving the experience of travel. They were fitted with spark-arresting chimneys to the vertical boilers.

The railway ran from the colonial capital in St. John's to Port aux Basques, a distance of 590 miles with branches from Whitbourne to Harbour Grace (the Harbour Grace Railway) and Whitbourne to the port of Placentia. Other branches ran to Bonavista, Heart's Content and Trepassey. The Harbour Grace line was later extended through Carbonear to Bay de Verde and there were several smaller branches, some of which were graded but rails were never installed. In 1923 the line was put under government control and it was with that administration that Sentinels did business.

The cars were used in branch line and commuter service around Corner Brook and St. John's, and lasted into the late 1930s. They were scrapped for the usual reasons: cost savings over conventional operations were not as much as anticipated. In addition they had adhesion difficulties in the winter.

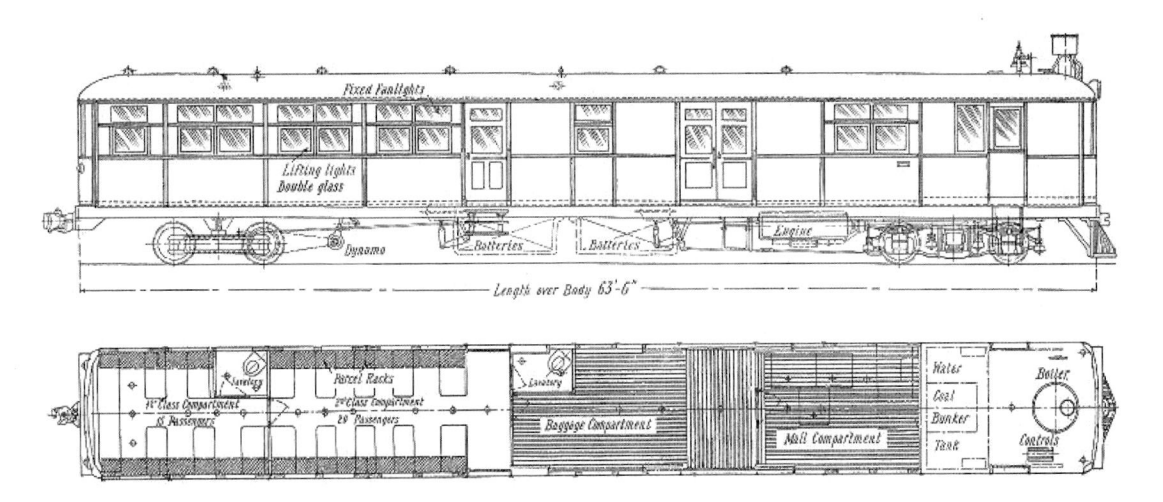

Above: Newfoundland cars "C", "D" & "F". Below: Rail Coach E, Newfoundland Railway.

Bengal Nagpur (Satpura Railway)

The Bengal Nagpur Railway is a largely broad-gauge Indian concern, of which the Satpura Railway is a narrow-gauge part. Today, much of the narrow-gauge has been converted; all are under the control of the South-Eastern Railway.

The Satpura lines of the South Eastern Railway covering large areas of Central India was the biggest network of 2ft 6in gauge lines on Indian Railways. The first major line (228km) ran northwards from Gondia to Nainpur and Jabalpur and was opened between 1903 and 1905. Another line from Nainpur was opened to Chhindwara (99km) in the west and to Mandla Fort (42km) in the east in 1904 and a long 236km southward section was opened from Gondia to Nagpur via Nagbhir. A connecting line (142km) from Itwari near Nagpur to Chhindwara was completed in 1913. Various branches brought the total length of the Satpura lines to 1005km.

Sentinel railmotors works Nos. 6104, 6126, 6127 were all delivered to the 2ft 6in gauge railway in 1926. They were the first narrow-gauge railmotors to be built with the short-lived vertical cylinder arrangement, although they continued to be chain-driven. The poor quality photo of works No. 6104 shows that it was a three-piece unit with the central driven section articulated to two short passenger cars, the only example of this arrangement that has come to light so far.

North Western Railway, Peru

At the beginning of 1927 a vertical-cylinder car was delivered to Ferrocarril del Noroeste del Perú. This was works No. 6289 of 3ft gauge, an articulated two-cylinder car. The railway ran for 194km from Ancon to Huacho with branches adding to the length. It was built and operated by an American company, and seems to have largely served the sugar industry. In 1928 a new branch of 46 km to

Works No. 6104. (courtesy Anthony R. Thomas)

Supe and Barranca was built and it was at this date also that the company ordered Sentinel works No. 7564, which was delivered in 1929. This was one of the new six horizontal cylinder designs which dispensed with the need to articulate the driven end. Moreover, this car had two engines so that both bogies were driven, making it one of the "200-300 hp" vehicles. It was oil-fired, an option which was reckoned to facilitate working to high altitudes. The car could seat 38 passengers and the boiler was situated well back from the front of the car so that a luggage compartment could be placed between the driver's compartment and the saloon. The driving end included a 250 gallon oil tank and a 500 gallon water tank, the driver sitting at the right hand side. At the other end, Sentinel's drawing shows a "canteen", but the word "driver" is also placed there, so we can safely assume that the car could be driven from either end. The railway closed completely in 1964.

Brian Fawcett, who was for nearly twenty-five years in a senior position in the Central Railway of Peru, a standard-gauge line of which the Nor-Oeste was a subsidiary, writes interestingly about the Sentinels. As the Central had some, too, he may well have had the standard-gauge in mind, but his remarks still throw interesting light on the cars:

"The steam railcar had the advantage of being designed for its purpose. It was sturdy, reliable, and familiar to roundhouse forces trained in the lore of steam traction. The drawbacks were that two men were required in the cabs, and that engine power was not sufficient for heavy grades. Its first cost was of course considerably more than that of the home-made body on a commercial truck chassis; but then, its passenger capacity was also considerably greater. Where the nature of the line permitted, and the volume of traffic required it, the steam railcar was a winner. Those early chain-driven or cardan shaft steam jobs of the 1920s performed a magnificent service. In the next decade ambitious attempts were made to adapt them for one-man operation by providing automatic oil firing and boiler feed arrangements. Instead of a fireman, drivers frequently had the enforced company of a fitter or electrician struggling head downwards in infernal temperatures with relays, valve adjustments and coordinated functions. The reliable old simple engines were re-placed with small axle-mounted compound engines rotating at such high speeds that when anything gave – as it all too often did – the whole works exploded into tiny fragments! The promising start to serious steam railcar development dissolved in chaos. Eyes turned hopefully to the diesel engine, now coming to the fore in other parts of the sub-continent and elsewhere."

One of the earliest non-articulated cars, this Peruvian example (works No. 7564) had two six-cylinder engines. This picture shows the car as having steps at the doorways so that passengers could enter without the benefit of platforms. (courtesy Ray Ellis)

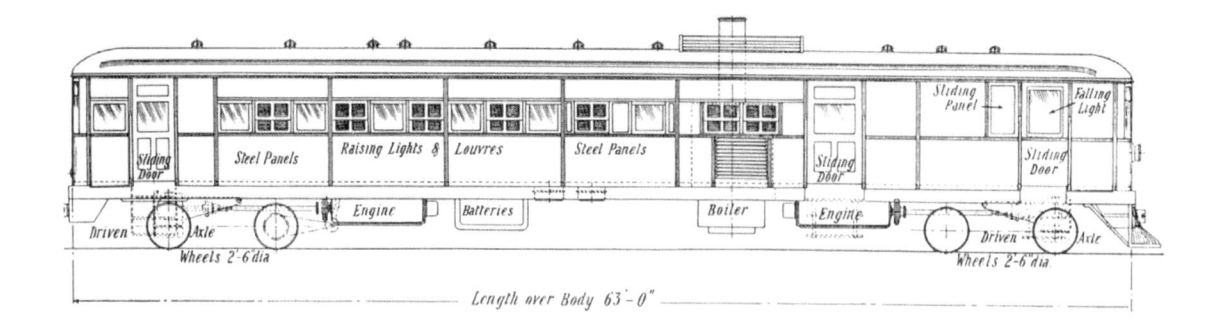

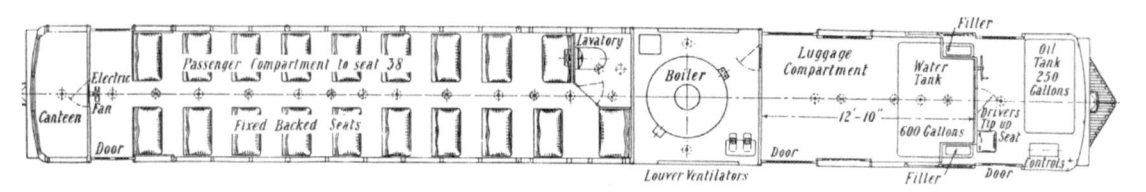

This diagram, from the 1932 catalogue, shows the car pictured on page 23

His comments seem to cut across the experience of, say, Sri Lanka (Ceylon), where the six-cylinder machines outlasted the two cylinder ones by a long way. He comments, also, that high altitudes, where water boils at a lower temperature, made steam railcars very poor performers.

It is interesting to note that the standard gauge Tacna to Arica Railway, which runs across the border from Peru to Chile, has at least one Sentinel rail motor converted to diesel which was operating in 2009 and may well still be in service.

Barsi Light Railway, India

This 2ft 6in gauge railway, a glorified tramway, ran from Miraj to Latur, then several different territories but now all part of Maharashtra state. It covered a total of 300km, but has become a victim of "Project Unigauge" which aims to convert Indian Railways to their standard (broad) gauge, so much of it has gone. The railway was the brainchild of the English railway genius E.R. Calthrop and it had a connection to the Bengal Nagpur lines (see above). Until 1954 it was owned and run by the English Barsi Light Railway Company.

Competition from road vehicles was beginning to prove troublesome, particularly on the comparatively short Pandharpur-Kurduwadi-Barsi Town sections, and to combat this two Sentinel steam motor coaches were purchased in 1925 for £3995 each. These were of the small group which had two-cylinder vertical engines and chain drive. As an alternative, three Sentinel locomotives were also purchased together with light-weight carriages supplied by Leeds Forge. A report commissioned to examine chaotic bus competition in the 1930s stated "Sentinel locomotives have done much to retain passengers to the (Barsi) railway." The same report adds (though it probably refers to a standard gauge railway): "On some Divisions Sentinel coaches have been used, though not with very great success, chiefly owing to mechanical defects, limited speed and limited seating capacity."

A later note says that at March 31 1940 the stock included one Sentinel 0-4-0 and one railcar and in June 1941 the Agent was instructed 'to accept any reasonable offer for the two Sentinels'.

The railcars, Sentinels 6341/42 of 1927, Barsi Light Railway class E, were numbered 28/27 (in that order).

Ceylon Government Railways

Railways in Ceylon (present day Sri Lanka) are mostly broad (5ft 6in) gauge, but some lines were built to the gauge of 2ft 6in. There were three narrow-gauge railways: Udapussellawa Railway (or UPR) - Nanuoya to Ragala via Nuwaraeliya; Kelani Valley Railway (or KV Line) - Colombo Maradana to Yatiyantota via Avissawella; and the Sabaragamuwa Railway Line - Awissavella to Opanayake. All are now abandoned or converted. The last two are often lumped together as the Kelani Valley (KV) line.

Sentinels supplied 33 Sentinel railmotors to the Ceylon Railways, but only six were of the narrow gauge. In 1927 they sent three of these: they were works Nos. 6391-3; probably 56 feet long, they had two vertical cylinders which drove the cars by means of chains. They were designated class V1 and numbered S28 – S30, later changed to 328-30. All worked on the KV line and 329 was withdrawn in 1944, the other two in 1946.

In 1927 the service on the Yatiyanthota branch of the Colombo to Opanake line consisted of two mixed and three railcar services each day. The railcars were allowed around an hour for the journey from the junction at Avissawella, a distance of about fifteen miles. The cars were undoubtedly also used on the KV main line.

No 331 in steam at Dematagoda shed, Colombo, in March 2006. (Robin Patrick)

The non-boiler end of 331 in Dematagoda shed in March 2006. (Robin Patrick)

They must have been successful, for works Nos. 7303-5 were built for the railway in 1928. These were of the later design, only 49ft 4in long and were the first narrow-gauge cars built with six horizontal cylinders set under the body, the system which allowed the cars to be built without articulation. These were designated class V2 (Abbott says R3), and numbered S31-33 (331-3). They seated 44 passengers, at first in two classes of 10 and 34, but later all in one.

V2 No. 331 survives, possibly in working order, though there is very little 2ft 6in gauge track left in Sri Lanka. It is at the Dematagoda (Colombo) locomotive shed, where a short length remains. Nos. 332 and 333 also exist, but in poor condition. Until the recent violent troubles in Sri Lanka, rail tour holidays often included a (short) ride on 331.

Iraq Railways

The Railway Gazette for February 3, 1928 summarised a report on the railways of Iraq. Some of Brigadier-General F. D. Hammond's remarks are worth our study:

The whole of the metre-gauge system, which both in respect of traffic and mileage is by far the more important (than the standard gauge), was built either during or after the war. Starting at Margil, where the deep-water wharves of the port of Basra are situated, the first section of the line traverses arid and practically waterless desert to Ur Junction, 125 miles distant. This section was hastily built behind the Army as it advanced; as the country was easy and lent itself to a surface line, little or no grading was done.

Above: Two views of the cab of 331. Below: interior of 332 in derelict condition. 29 January 2010. (James Waite)

The next section of 163 miles from Ur Junction to Hillah was not commenced until after the Armistice, and is consequently better graded with a maximum of 1 in 200. It also traverses better country, which has developed since the advent of the railway. Except for one short length, 50.lb. rails are used throughout, but again, unfortunately, of two different types. The bridges were originally of timber, but have now been replaced throughout by permanent structures.

The remainder of the metre-gauge system lies on the left bank of the Tigris. Starting at Baghdad North Station, it goes in a northerly direction to Qaraghan, mile 92, whence a short branch 17 miles long, leads to Khanaqin, seven miles from the Persian frontier and on the trade route to Kirnunnshah. From Qaraghan the main line proceeds in a north-westerly direction to the town of Kirkuk, mile 200....

The two metre-gauge systems are connected by a wagon ferry, crossing the Tigris a short distance up-stream of Baghdad. The ferry can transfer 72 four-wheeled vehicles in each direction in 11 hours. Difficulties have been experienced with it during time of floods....

A further measure which the Director of Railways has in hand is the purchase of a Sentinel coach for the Baqubah service. The Director calculates that its running expense will be approximately Rs 1s a mile against Rs. 4s. a mile for the ordinary train, which will enable him both to charge cheaper fares and give a better service. In the financial year 1927—28 he proposes, if funds permit, to purchase two Sentinel locomotives, capable of hauling two coaches apiece and to use them on similar work.

In 1920 the railways passed from military to civilian control and from April 1923, although continuing to belong to the British government, they were managed by the Iraqis.

In June 1927 works No. 6462 to metre gauge was supplied to the railway. It had two vertical cylinders, and since the locomotives supplied to Iraq were oil-burning, the railmotor may well have been also. Presumably, it was used on the Baqubah service, which would have been a 60km run from Baghdad along a line which probably no longer exists, but which was once the main route from Iraq to Iran. In view of what has happened in Iraq since that time, it is hardly surprising that we know almost nothing else about it.

Salvador Railways

In 1894, after years of largely unsuccessful railway building by a succession of companies, an English company, The Central American Public Works Company, was given the concession to complete the railway from Santa Ana to Santa Tecla in El Salvador in return for taking on the country's foreign debt. This company became the Salvador Railways Company which operated the Acajutla network.

Correspondence by the author with Central American rail enthusiast Allen Morrison suggests that there was no direct line between Santa Ana and Santa Tecla, and that, in any case, a vehicle as large as a Sentinel would be completely out of place on Salvadorian lines. So far, no record of any vehicle can be traced – and the 1932 Sentinel catalogue makes no mention of the Salvador Railway in its list of customers! However, the works list (as presented by Abbott) puts works No. 5484 as having been built in August 1926, before the previous seven works numbers. The list gives it as a two-cylinder 3ft gauge car – and there are 3ft gauge railways in El Salvador.

Nizam's State Railway, India

This metre gauge network (1899-1951) centred on Hyderabad was originally a series of lines owned by the Nizam of Hyderabad and worked by the Nizam's Guaranteed State Railway Company. When working passed to the Princely state in 1930 they were amalgamated as the metre gauge section of the NSR. Latterly, this was the core of the South Central Railway zone. The lines have almost all been converted to broad gauge.

Sentinel railmotors works numbers 6811-2 were supplied in 1927 to the metre gauge railway. Like their immediate predecessors, they were equipped with two vertical cylinders; they were, imaginatively, given the numbers 1 and 2. It seems possible that they operated on short hauls around Hyderabad and Secunderabad, but no firm information is available.

We know that the Nizam's State Railway was one of the first to experiment with diesel railcars, in 1939, just twelve years after the Sentinels arrived, but whether this shows that the steamers were so successful that they had to be augmented, or such a failure that they had to be replaced, remains to be seen.

Gold Coast Railway (in present-day Ghana)

Between 1898 and 1901 the mining town of Tarkwa was linked by a 41-mile railroad to Sekondi. In 1902 the line was extended 124 miles to Obuasi and in 1903 it was further extended 168 miles to Kumasi. Construction of the Accra-Kumasi railway, begun in 1905, was completed in 1923. A third railway, a branch linking Kade, a diamond mining centre, to Huni Valley was completed in 1926.

An interesting photo of an articulated car at the Metropolitan-Cammell works.

This railway, the Gold Coast Railway (now The Ghana Railways Corporation) is a 3ft 6in gauge system that has become almost derelict. Plans to re-gauge to standard gauge are in hand, but progress is slow and doubtful.

Works No. 6916 of December 1927 of 3ft 6in gauge was the last of the narrow-gauge two cylinder railmotors. At the Gold Coast Railway, it was given the number 1.

In 1928 works No. 7606 was supplied to the railway and given the number 2, then the next year two more railmotors were dispatched. Works Nos. 7975-6 were numbered 3 and 4.

Leopoldina Railway, Brazil

The Leopoldina Railway was based in Rio de Janeiro, and owned nearly two thousand miles of metre-gauge track making it the largest metre-gauge railway in the country. The records of the British parliament, *Hansard*, for 28 July 1931 show that a question in the House about the railway revealed that the headquarters were in London. The railway carried a lot of suburban traffic in large conurbations, but it also served far-flung areas with steep gradients and tight curves. It was a railway of long trains and powerful locomotives, so the Sentinels seem almost incongruous in the context. In fact, the first of them was not for general service at all.

In March 1928 the Shrewsbury factory built works number 7420, a metre-gauge car with a single engine of six horizontal cylinders driving the front bogie of a rigid structure. This was unusual in that it was designed as an inspection car. At one end it had a day saloon with comfortable chairs and fixed tables, whilst a pantry and a bathroom were placed either side of the almost central boiler compartment which included the coal bunker. A side corridor led past these to two two-berth sleeping compartments. The whole was completed by a driver's compartment at each end.

Outwardly, this car conformed to the traditional Sentinel shape; the company must have been very pleased with it as they included both a photograph and a drawing in the 1932 catalogue! In Brazil it was given the number 500-A.

In 1936 the railway obtained two more Sentinel railmotors; they were works Nos. 9265-6 and they seem to have been similar mechanically to the original car, although they were oil-fired. Otherwise, however, they were quite different; by this time Metropolitan-Cammell had adopted a much more streamlined body shape (quite similar in outline to the first generation of diesel multiple units) and the saloons of these vehicles were designed to seat 32 passengers, not for inspection purposes. These units were numbered 501-B and 502-B.

Palestine Railway

Palestine Railways was a government-owned railway company that ran all public railways in the League of Nations mandate territory of Palestine from 1920 until 1948. Its main line linked El Kantara in Egypt with Haifa. Branches served Jaffa, Jerusalem, Acre and the Jezreel Valley, but the section we are interested in was to the Hejaz (or Hedjaz) Railway gauge of 1050mm.

The Hejaz Railway ran from Damascus to Medina, through the Hejaz region of Arabia, with a branch line to Haifa, on the Mediterranean Sea. The Jezreel Valley railway was built at the beginning of the 20th century and connected Haifa with the rest of the Hejaz railway, its last stop within the Palestine Mandate borders being al-Hamma. After many failed attempts, the final planning and construction lasted four years. The railway was inaugurated on October 15, 1905 and operated until the middle of the 20th century.

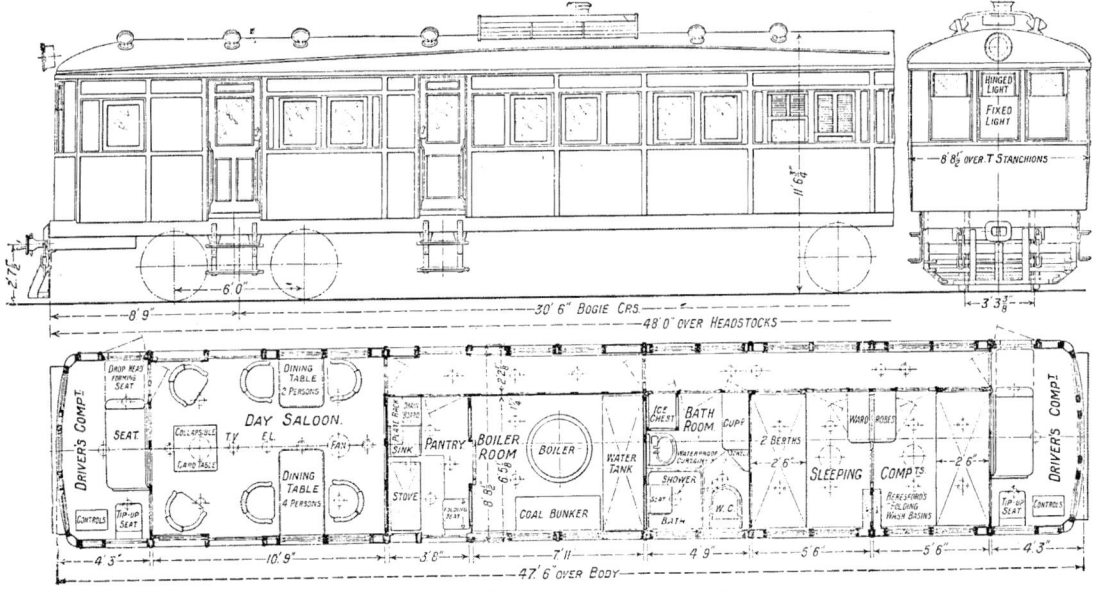

Top: Leopoldina Inspection Car. (Sentinel 1932 catalogue, courtesy Ray Ellis) above: diagram of the Inspection Car from the 1932 catalogue.

After the Israeli declaration of independence in 1948, the line suffered much damage, and though there was some use from Haifa to Afula until about 1951, the stock was then completely dismantled, so nothing significant remains today.

In the 1929 Palestine Railways "Administrative Report for the Year ending 31st. December 1929", on page 11, we find: *Sentinel Cammell Steam Cars. Two Sentinel-Cammell Steam Cars for the Palestine Railways and two for the Hijaz Railway, costing approximately £P 7,000 each, arrived from England early in 1929. Due, to some extent, to the quality of water at the majority of watering stations, injector trouble has been frequent in the operation of these cars, but it is hoped to lessen this difficulty by substituting feed pumps for injectors. Now it has been established that these* cars are popular with the public, it will be necessary to consider the purchase of additional cars as the present number does not provide any reserve for repairs. Developments in the use of the Diesel type engine are being watched with a view to possible adoption should they prove successful under similar conditions to those obtaining in Palestine.*

So they were popular in Palestine! The injector trouble, however, is a problem which occurs in the notes of a number of railways, and, although it is attributed to a variety of causes, this seems to indicate a weakness in the design. Even standard-gauge LNER cars suffered from this problem.

In *The Hedjaz Railway* (Tourret Publishing, 1989, ISBN 0-905878-05-1), R. Tourret writes: *In 1929 four Sentinel-Cammell double articulated steam railcars were ordered by the Crown Agents for the Colonies to the requirements of Major H.A. Catching for service on the P.R.... Two, numbered SC1 and SC2, were built for the 4ft 8½in gauge and two, numbered SC11 & SC12, for the 1.050m gauge. The bodies and underframes were identical, so that by changing bogies any of the cars could be converted to the other gauge, the headstocks being arranged to take either side buffers for standard gauge or the centre buffing and drawgear of the 1.050m gauge... The steps were arranged so as to be suitable for both standard and 1,050mm lines.*

The outside of the body was painted in grey cellulose enamel (the standard gauge cars were chocolate). Later, the 1.050m cars were painted an olive colour. They were laid aside in spring 1939 and converted into unpowered third-class twin-coach units.

Works Nos. 7434-5 to 1050mm gauge were in fact built for The Palestine Railway in March 1928. These were double-articulated (two-car) units with a single engine of six cylinders. As Tourret says, they were numbered 11 and 12 by the railway and are said to be the only new trains provided for the narrow gauge during the time of the mandate. A photograph shows one of them at Haifa station on 30th March 1930 and a list dated 1944 shows that both cars still existed at that time, though one was in store. Other sources suggest that they were withdrawn to be converted to unpowered use in 1939. It seems likely that they worked the branch to Acre or, just possibly, the lines to Afuleh, Samakh (for connection to the Hejaz Railway), Nablus or Tulkarm.

The *Railway Gazette* for February 1 1929 is worth quoting at length as it is a rare insight into the cars and much of its detail must apply to other cars as well. Of the Palestine cars, it tells us: *The interior accommodation comprises a first-class compartment with seating for 12 passengers, two third-class compartments seating 35 and 42 passengers, and a small luggage compartment. The two lower-class compartments are situated at the articulated end of the bogies and communication is provided between the two by means of a closed vestibule. There are hinged doors in all partitions affording communication from one end of the car to the other. Lavatory accommodation is provided for both classes.*

In the first-class compartments the seating is of the transverse type the seat backs being fixed. The woodwork is polished teak throughout the compartment, and the seats are upholstered in blue leather of the railway company's standard shade. The compartment is fitted with oxidised parcel racks and a powerful electric roof fan. In the lower-class compartments the seating is also transverse the seats having reversible backs and being of the lath and space type in varnished pitch-pine.

The interior panels throughout the car are of 'Sundeala' except in the lavatories which are lined with 'Calbanite' panels. The window openings in all compartments are provided with raising lights and louvres all framed in teak. Monarch roof ventilators are fitted in all passenger and luggage compartments.

One of the Palestinian units at Haifa Station.

The lighting installation is of the Pyle National type with a 1,500 watt turbo-generator arranged at the rear of the engine cab. Suitable lighting is provided in all passenger and luggage compartments, lavatories, driving compartments etc. The car is also provided with a powerful headlight mounted at each end of the car, together with tail and indicator lights to the railway company's standard requirements. Electric signal bells are fitted in each driver's compartment with a push-button operating each at the opposite end of the car. A steam whistle is mounted on the cab roof at the leading end of the car, operative from both drivers' compartments.

Efficient ventilation of the boiler compartment is ensured by a ventilating "deck" fitted on the roof, and louvres in the front side panels. Furthermore, the roof of the cab is lined with "Sundeala" at the sides, the end windows having hinged fanlights and the cab side doors being provided with falling windows. A sliding body at the rear of the cab sides gives further ventilation when required.

The outside of the body is finished with a special sprayed-on cellulose enamel; the normal-gauge cars are finished in the railway company's standard chocolate shade and the narrow-gauge cars in grey.

It is interesting, and possibly unique, that all four cars ordered were capable of being converted to the alternate gauge, but it emphasises the fact that many narrow-gauge Sentinels were built to the (British) standard loading gauge. Of the standard gauge cars, 1 and 2, Paul Cotterell in *The Railways of Palestine and Israel* (Tourret Publishing 1984: ISBN 0-905878-04-3) reports "In practice, their drawbacks tended to outweigh the theoretical advantages. The main problem was that they were weak and had limited capacity." His diagram of the standard-gauge cars surely reflects the narrow-gauge ones as well; they had two "native latrines" and a first-class lavatory! The first-class was naturally as far from the boiler as possible (i.e. in the No. 2 end of the trailer car).

From the Israel Railways General Manager's Report for the Years 1948/49-1951-52 we learn that the two Sentinels were on the list of existing stock but had been removed because, along with many other items, they were "damaged between 31/3/47 and 15/5/48". They do not appear on any list of Israel railways coaching stock.

By the courtesy of Mr Chen Melling, deputy manager of the Israel Railway Museum, we have the following:

Above: official photograph of the narrow-gauge Palestinian articulated cars. (courtesy: J. Bennett archive)

Below: Crash between HR railcar and 'Egged' bus in Affula. (Benny Haspel collection)

PR Annual Reports

According to the 1929 annual report, the four sets entered service during Feb-Mar 1929 and cost some £P7000 (Palestine Pounds) each. The report states that "Due, to some extent, to the quality of water at the majority of watering stations, injector trouble has been frequent in the operation of these cars, but it is hoped to lessen this difficulty by substituting feed pumps for injectors." The cars are reported as being popular with the public, and it is suggested that the purchase of more is to be considered, perhaps Diesel-engined (if such proves viable in the local conditions), as there is currently no reserve for repair.

The 1931-2 report (by this time the local financial year was changed to start on 1 April) describes a 'malicious derailment' of one of the NG sets, which took place at 21:30 on 22nd October 1931 between Beisan and Jisr

Palestine Railways statistics 1931-2. Courtesy Chen Melling.

El Miami and was caused by "… the malicious removal of a rail from the track by some persons who have not been traced." The car narrowly escaped falling down the bank and so there were only a few minor injuries to the passengers. According to the report, "Owing to the light construction of the body work, the salvaging of the car, which was badly damaged, was a difficult and delicate operation." It was eventually repaired at a cost of £P 346 and returned to traffic on December 28 1932.

The next notable references to the Sentinel-Cammell railcars comes in the 1936-7 report, where it is stated that during the year, new boilers were installed in both narrow gauge sets and in one of the standard gauge ones. Also, one of the SG sets was damaged in the disturbances which started that year.

The annual report for 1938-9 (the last one published before the end of WWII) states that there was a reduction of almost 40% in running kilometrage of the railcars (presumably of both gauges combined) which reduced the numbers of running repairs necessary.

The next report was published in 1947 and summarized the years 1942-6. The stock lists in that report state that the standard-gauge sets were converted to locomotive-hauled coaches (by removal of boiler etc.) and the narrow gauge ones were "Laid Aside". Nevertheless, the 1946-7 report (the last published by Palestine Railways), published shortly thereafter, shows that during the year 1945-6 one light repair was performed on a narrow gauge set. The repairs table for the year 1946-7 shows that both sets are "Awaiting Repair" and that one of them is "Stabled".

PR Timetables

The 1934 and 1935 timetables show railcar running on two narrow-gauge sections – Haifa–Kiryat Haim–Acre and Haifa–Meshek Yagour-Samakh. The former section had seven return workings, four of them only to Kiryat Haim, the latter had one short and one long return working per day. All workings started and finished in Haifa station (today Haifa East) where there was also a narrow-gauge running shed (which today acts as the Museum's main hall). As these are public timetables, it's impossible to see whether each section was due to be served by the same set for the whole day, though the timings allow for two switch opportunities in Haifa.

The next public timetable to differentiate between loco-hauled and railcar-operated trains is the 1938 one. In it, the railcars operate over the same lines, but only in what might be termed 'suburban' workings, i.e. only covering the sections close to Haifa, with six return workings to Kiryat Motzkin (an additional stop a short distance north of Kiryat Haim) and two return workings to Kiryat Haroshet, another new stop, this time two stations further than Meshek Yagour. Again there is a chance for a switch at Haifa East.

Starting from the 1942 timetable there is but a single planned return working per weekday, which up till 1944 is between Samakh and Haifa East, with the over-night stay in Samakh (which also had a running shed, although smaller). The 1943 public timetable states that the accommodation is 3rd class only, which means the 1st class accommodation has been dispensed with by this time.

Working timetable 4 of 1 November 1945 shows a single railcar return working, this time between Haifa East and Beisan (today Bet Shean), and this is termed "Haifa-Beisan Local Service" despite Beisan being quite far away from Haifa and much nearer Samakh. In fact, the timings suggest that again the overnight stay was made at nearby Samakh. By the amended Working timetable 4 of 23 July 1946 the single working is again scheduled to go from Samakh to Haifa East and back. It should be noted that by this time the attacks on the railway had risen to such levels as to make timetabling more of an academic occupation, and beginning in late 1947 the situation became pretty chaotic until the end of Israel's War of Independence in 1949.

Eventual Fate

No use is known to have been made of the four railcars by Israel Railways (IR) but in Harakevet Magazine, item No. 47:7(i), Paul Cotterell describes the consideration given in 1953 by IR to conversion of the narrow gauge sets to standard gauge (the remaining narrow gauge sections finally closed in 1951) and possible installation of Diesel engines in all four sets. Sentinel's reply to the suggestion was that it was not practical using Diesel engines at their disposal and so nothing came of this. In the same issue, as item No. 47:7(b), Paul wrote that according to Israel Railways management file Peh/24/6, set SC11's boiler (No. 1377) and motor bogie were sold in 1954, but the sale was cancelled at the request of the Israel Nautical College in Acre, who received the items instead in May 1955. Incidentally, this institution resides to this day at the location of the Hijaz Railway Acre station, so the railcars remains would have felt at home there. Unfortunately, nothing remains today of either the railcars or the station.

Bombay, Baroda and Central India Railway

The metre gauge network (1907-51) was originally the Rajputana-Malwa State Railway, which was amalgamated with the BBCI after the latter became state owned in 1906. The company continued to work the lines until 1942. Its main line was Ahmedabad (Ahmadabad) to Delhi, later part of the Western Railway zone of IR. The lines have now mostly been converted to broad gauge. The Indore-Mhow route was part of a straggling metre gauge line from Ajmer to Khandwa. Indore is an old town, the capital of one of the Princely states. Mhow (allegedly, but very unreliably, standing for Military Headquarters of War) was a major military centre and was very busy, especially in 1943. (I am indebted to Keith Scholey for this and other Indian information.)

Sentinels supplied works Nos. 7584-6 in 1928 ; like the Palestine cars, these were articulated two-car units with a single six cylinder engine, making them what the company called "The 100-150 HP Articulated Rail Car". The boiler, bunker and controls at the leading end were followed by the guard's compartment. Next came a Ladies' compartment to seat 12 (the ladies had the hottest seats in the train!). The leading car had 36 more third class seats, and the trailer had another 56. A twelve-seat first class compartment completed the passenger accommodation, after which was the second driving compartment.

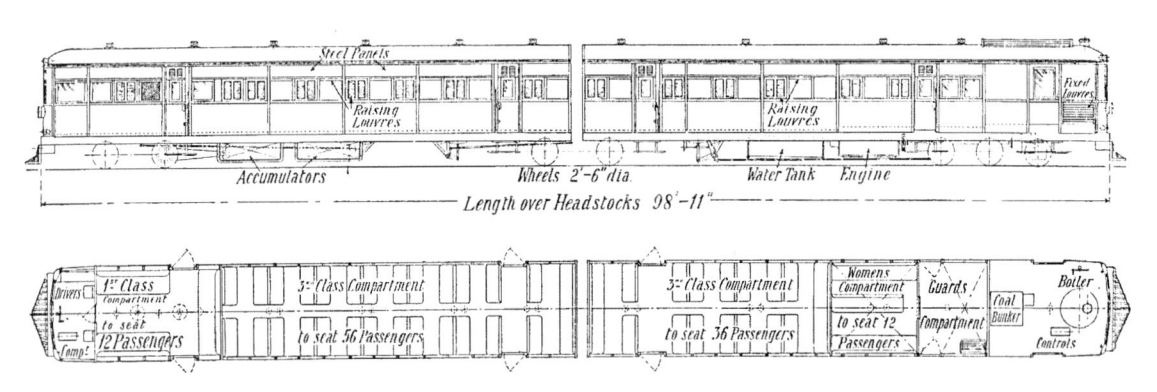

BB&CI Rly: official drawing. The caption states: 116 passengers in four compartments.

BB&CI Rly: from the Indian State Railways Magazine for October 1930. (Ray Ellis)

It is not yet known on which parts of the system the Sentinels were used, but an anonymous traveller wrote: "The Indian Bradshaw of May 1943 gave a Sentinel Service between Indore and Mhow twice daily in each direction but I never saw any sign of it," so it seems likely that the former Rajputana-Malwa Railway lines were the destination of the cars.

Nigerian Railways

Nigerian Railways was a network of 3,505 kilometres (2,178 miles) of single track lines, all of 1,067 mm (3ft 6in) gauge. Much has fallen into decay, but in 1928 it was a network that helped to open up the country to trade.

Sentinel supplied works No. 7607 in 1928, works No. 8144 in 1929 and, almost incredibly, works Nos. 9553-4 in 1953. They were all provided with six-cylinder engines, but no more information about them has yet come to light. Undoubtedly, the appearance of the later ones was much more streamlined than the earlier as by this time Metropolitan-Cammell had adopted a different body shape.

Taking water on the Nigerian Railways - from Railway Gazette 1933

Tanganyika Railway (in present-day Tanzania)

In Tanganyika, the Germans started construction of the metre-gauge Central Line from Dar es Salaam in February 1904. This line eventually reached Kigoma on Lake Tanganyika in 1914. A branch line was built from Tabora to Mwanza on the southern shore of Lake Victoria, being completed in 1928. A line from Tanga was commenced in 1899 reaching Mombo in 1904. The line then headed for Mount Kilimanjaro, reaching Moshi in 1911. A link line was constructed in 1924 connecting it to the Uganda railway at Voi. In 1929 the line was continued to Arusha. Another link line was constructed as late as 1963 to connect the northern and central lines. The other Tanganyikan branches were from Manyoni to Kinyangiri, built in 1934 but lifted in 1947, the Mpanda branch in 1949, and the Kilosa-Kidatu branch completed in 1965.

Sentinel works Nos. 7638-9 were supplied in 1929 and were numbered 51-2. Works No. 9232 of 1935 seems not to have been sent out to Tanganyika, as works No. 9334 was a modification of this in 1937, when the car seems to have been supplied (see below).

The first two of these Tanganyikan cars were bought by the management in order to challenge the competition from increasingly efficient road traffic. They were 100-150 hp cars (i.e. with a single six-cylinder engine and vertical boiler). It was believed that the railmotors would be rather cheaper to operate than the traditional locomotive-hauled trains. They had eight first-, eight second- and forty third-class seats and they were rigid vehicles with one underfloor six-cylinder engine. Lavatories were provided, though probably not for third class.

They were first put into service on the Moshi – Arusha service at its inception, but there turned out not to be enough traffic for the service provided, so they were transferred to the more heavily used Tanga – Korogwe section. They are reported to have been so popular and successful here that the authorities ordered a third vehicle.

Here, some uncertainty intrudes. Ramaer, in his excellent article in *Continental Railway Journal*, suggests that it took Sentinels three years (1935-8) to deliver this vehicle. The works list, however,

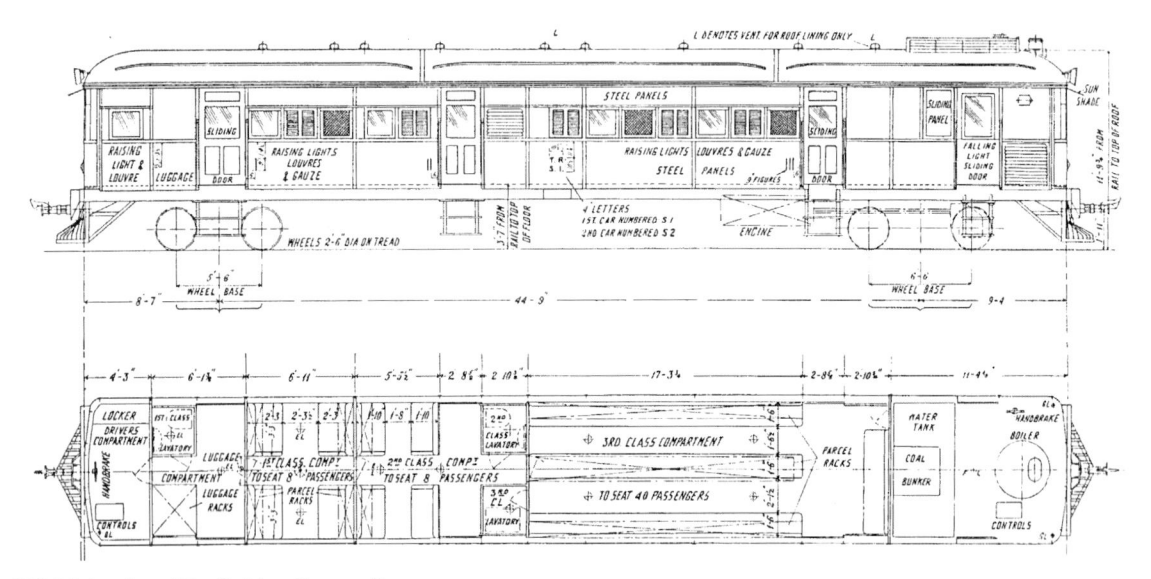

Official drawing of the first two Tanganyikan cars.

Tanganyika Railways metre gauge Sentinel-Cammell Steam Railcar No. 1or 2. (Continental Railway Journal.)

suggests that it was completed in 1935 as a vertical-boilered, single-engined car and modified at Shrewsbury in 1937. Moreover, that list shows it to be of 3ft 6in or Cape Gauge. Ramaer goes on to say that this car seated eight second- and sixty third-class passengers, with lavatories for each class. In this car the boiler was placed between the accommodation for the different classes.

Ramaer also reports that a Sentinel locomotive was re-geared and used experimentally to haul a coach on the Tabora – Mwanza line in the period before the new railmotor was delivered.

In a follow-up article in Continental Railway Journal No. 82, Summer 1990, compiled from information supplied by Henry Gunston and John Mulchings (Assistant Archivist, The Sentinel Trust), who themselves incorporated information obtained from the Crown Agents, the late John MacLagan and Brian Yonge, much is explained:

Records of The Sentinel Trust indicate that the two earlier cars carried Sentinel works numbers 7638/9 and that they were numbered S1 and S2 on arrival in Tanganyika. These cars underwent major overhauls around 1934 when the 1st class section was converted to 2nd class, and the existing 2nd class accommodation to 3rd (with lavatory removed) giving seats for an additional ten 3rd class passengers and making 50 in all. Although the cars gave excellent service and the concept was sound, the usual body problems found in Sentinel-Cammell cars became evident during overhaul. The body construction was weak, causing distortion, principal failings being inadequate bracing of door pillars and window frames, compounded by the roof being too heavy for its supports. (The same problems manifested themselves at Darlington as at Dar-es-Salaam). Remedial work was carried out during overhaul and must have been satisfactory as one vehicle, in coach form, has survived until recently and may still exist. The two cars were named about 1934, one being "Mwendo Mbio" (Swahili for "Go like the Wind") and the other "Mamboni Na Sasa" ("The Last Word").

The EAR&H (East African Railways and Harbours) Annual Report of 1951 confirms conversion of cars 1 and 2 to third class coaches, and in 1953 they were in use on the Tanga line carrying numbers TB (for Third Bogie, Side Door – not corridor as quoted in the original article) 140/1. By 1956 they had been renumbered to TB 3040/1, with 91 and 90 passenger seats respectively, but by 1966 only 3040 remained on the rolling stock list. TB 3040 was seen in Nairobi carriage sidings in mid-1968, possibly awaiting withdrawal as by early 1970, when seen at Naivasha, it carried the inscription "Engineering Department, Signal & Telecommunications", having been converted for signal maintenance staff accommodation. It still carried the passenger plum and cream livery with black roof, and the number TB 3040. In August 1972 at Dagoretti (again on the Nairobi–Nakuru line in Kenya) it had an overall maroon livery and a new number SLB (for Staff Labour Van Bogie) 117058. By February 1985 the livery had been changed to green with an aluminium/silver roof, but the original wording of the text had been retained. It seems quite likely that SLB 117058 is still in use today along the Nakuru line out of Nairobi, more than 60 years after its birth in September 1928.

The third railcar incorporated modified body construction intended to eradicate the defects of the first pair. It was slightly shorter overall to permit a locomotive to haul or propel it with safety over main-line and station crossovers in the event of total failure, something not possible with the first two cars because of their length. This car (allocated Sentinel Job No. 9232) was ordered in August 1935 and was intended to have an axle-mounted engine with two 6in x 6in cylinders, but development of this caused much delay and it was eventually abandoned. This resulted in the order being re-issued by Sentinel on 27th May 1937 under Job No. 9334, with the usual 6-cylinder engine and cardan shaft drive. Delivery, originally required by May 1936, finally took place in the autumn of 1937. This car was named "Mwendo Wa Raha" ("Go with Joy").

Note: The East African Railways and Harbours Corporation evolved from the Uganda Railway in Kenya and Uganda and the railways of Tanganyika (later Tanzania) between World War I and 1977 when the East African Community dissolved.

Of course, it is possible that works No. 9232 was built to metre gauge and that the works list is wrong (it often is, and the version provided by Abbott does not include 9232 at all), but it is interesting to speculate that it may have been built to 3ft 6in at a time when gauge conversion was contemplated (as it was from time to time) and that Shrewsbury had to change it to metre gauge later. The mention of bodywork problems in the above extract is interesting as it assumes that these

Tanganyika Railways metre gauge Sentinel as a Staff Labour Van No. SLB 117058, at Naivasha, Kenya, in February 1985. (Continental Railway Journal.)

Above: the official works photo of the third Tanganyikan machine; this clearly shows the change of body shape used for the later cars. Below: official drawing of Tanganyika 3

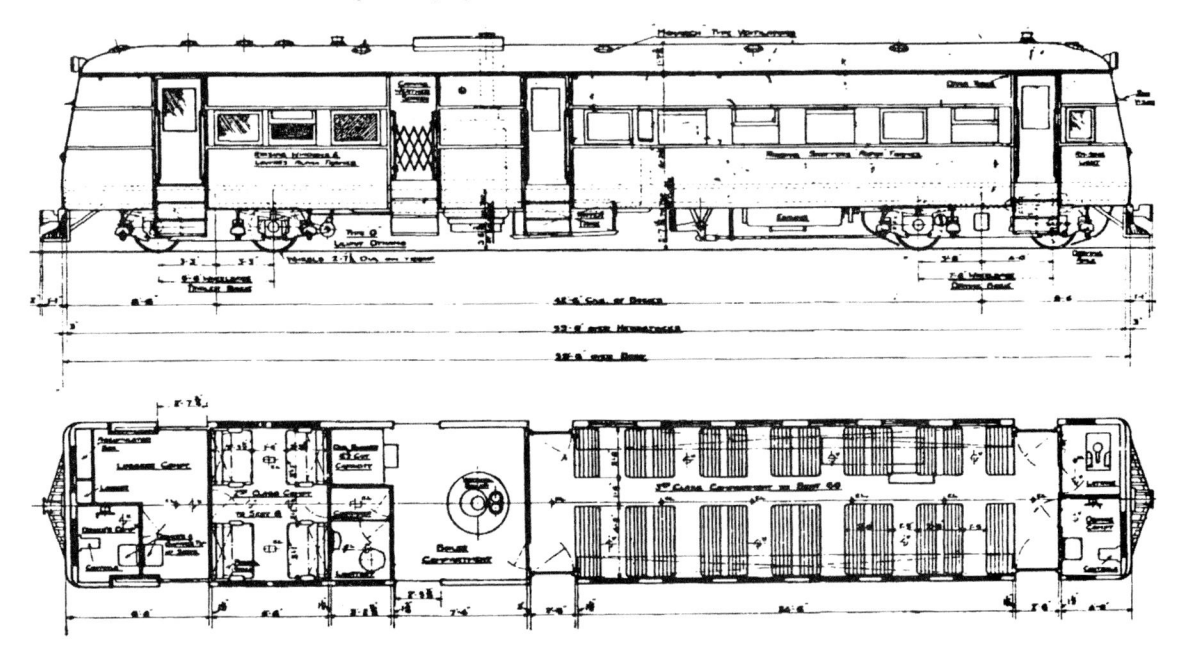

were common (see the reference to "Darlington") but no other such reports have come to light and it seems to be generally accepted that Metropolitan-Cammell built very well. The axle-mounted, two-cylinder engine mentioned appears unique also.

Federated Malay States Railway

The Federated Malay States Railways (FMSR) was a consolidated railway operator in British Malaya (present day Peninsular Malaysia and Singapore) during the first half of the 20th century. Named after the then recently formed Federated Malay States in 1896 and founded five years after the formation of the federation, the company acquired railways that were developed separately in various parts of Malaya, and oversaw the largest expansion and integration of the colonies' rail network encompassing the Federated Malay States, the Unfederated Malay States (except

Trengganu) and the Straits Settlements, with lines spanning from Singapore to the south to Padang Besar to the north.

The metre-gauge railway had had some experience of steam rail cars built by Sentul works in Malaya. Believed to be inspired by the railmotors of the Great Western Railway (UK), these railcars were based on a conventional 0-6-0 chassis. Two-car sets were planned in 1914 and four had been completed by 1917. It is not known if any more were built. They seem to have been small 0-6-0 locomotives fitted within conventional coach bodies.

In 1930 the Federated Malay States Railway bought, through the Crown Agents, a Sentinel unit (works No. 7781) which had been built at Shrewsbury in 1929. This was a two-car unit with two four-wheel driving bogies, one at the boiler end and one in the centre; the two cars were articulated (the central bogie supported the inner ends of both cars) and was in effect a steam multiple unit which was able to seat 107 people in second- and third-class sections. It was designated SR1 and had second- (some sources say first-) class seating with leather seats and ceiling fans. The third class had slatted wood seats and no fans. Sentinel's standard three-window cab front was provided and the unit had articulated control gear to enable control from either end.

Five more, broadly similar sets, (works Nos. 8538-42 and designated class SR2) were delivered two years later. They all had 2-axle power bogies and 6 cylinders. The leather seats were replaced with woven cane. A further six pairs (works Nos. 9267-9 and 9295-7 designated SR3) were supplied in

A later FMSR unit. The terraced houses in the background, the dual-gauge track, the obviously English figures, the overhead electric wires, the telegraph poles and the fact that the unit is in grey all persuade one that this shot was taken at the Cammell-Laird test track. (courtesy Anthony R. Thomas).

1938 with a larger boiler and 3-axle bogie, extra seating and a toilet in each coach. It seems that these cars were numbered SR1- 12 at first. This would have resulted in a vehicle of class SR2 being numbered SR3! Post war, however, they were designated class 25 (SR1 & SR2) and class 26 (SR3) and numbered 251.01, 252.01 – 05 and 261.01 – 06. All were named: 251.01 *Langhar* also recorded as *Sri Kanchil*; 252.01 *Raja Wali*; 252.02 *Raja Udang*; 252.03 *Tekukor*; 252.04 *Serindit*; 252.05 *Chenderawaseh*; 261.01 *Sri Laju*; 261.02 *Sri Lanchar*; 261.03 *Sri Lajak*; 261.04 *Enggang*; 261.05 *Kijang*; 261.06 *Seladang*.

These were really substantial units as the Malaysian metre-gauge loading gauge is huge by British standards, so it is likely that these units had even more in common with the standard gauge cars than the others discussed here. In fact, the loading gauge in Malaya is actually larger than the standard-gauge British equivalent.

They seem to have done sterling service, being used intensively. They were not confined to local services but were also used on longer distance stopping passenger services. The 1939 working timetable shows that they were doing up to 200 miles daily on services based around Kuala Lumpur, Ipoh, Seremban, Gemas and Krai. They seem to have been running at around 20mph although official tables show that they were permitted to run at a top speed of 45 mph on most lines!

Four of the SR2 and three SR3 were in the Kuala Lumpur area in 1955 with 252.05 active at that time. By 1958 only one Sentinel working appears in the timetable; it operated on the Sultan Street Ampang branch.

Western Australian Government Railway

Presumably, the management of the Western Australian Government Railway (WAGR) had heard of the Sentinel in use on the Commonwealth Railway (see above). Because of, or perhaps in spite of, this, they ordered works No. 8189 which was delivered in January 1930 to this 3ft 6in gauge railway.

This car operated mainly on the South-west suburban line between Perth and Armadale, a distance of twenty miles. Although it was a vertical boilered, single-engined (100 – 150 hp) car, it sometimes pulled a trailer coach; for this purpose it was equipped with a gated corridor connection at the No. 2 end, although it was capable of being driven from that end if required. It ran at 30.7 (sic) mph, but was reputed to be capable of 60! In common with many of the later cars, it had condensing apparatus on the roof.

In 1936 it had to be withdrawn because of big-end failure, but a railway report records that this was not the fault of the manufacturer. It may have been careless driving.

During the 1940s it was used for special tours; since it was equipped with a lavatory and seating for over forty passengers it was ideally suited to the work. In 1959 it was converted into a track recording car, and all its traction equipment removed and scrapped. Today, it is preserved under cover at the Boyanup Railway Museum near Bunbury, although at the time of writing the museum is closed.

At first this car was painted all over Indian Red, but in 1940 this was changed to green and cream (why is it that so many railmotors were painted in this livery?). In 1951 an eau de nil strip above the windows was added. It even had yellow safety stripes for a brief period.

WAGR Sentinel in green and cream livery. (WAGR)

Deli Spoorweg Maatschappij, Sumatra

In 1881 Jacob Theodoor Cremer from the Netherlands Trading Company initiated the establishment of the Deli Spoorweg Maatschappij (Deli Railroad Company) or DSM for transportation of the tobacco from the plantations to the harbour. In October 1883 construction was started, in July 1886 the first line Laboean - Medan was opened and in February 1888 the line Laboean - Belawan, the new harbour. In total 335 miles of 3ft 6in gauge track was built. To this system, in 1930, Sentinel sent works No. 8383, a vertical-boilered, single engined car.

Tasmanian Government Railway

The TGR were certain that they needed a kind of railcar for services on branch lines around the system. In the mid 1920s they experimented with petrol-driven cars, but these proved inadequate for the job (in Tasmania the branches were often very long) and from 1931 nine Sentinels were brought into use. As we have seen, Australian railway personnel went to Jersey to see The Pioneer

The catalogue caption states: 100-15-hp oil fired single type rail car hauling trailer coach and brake van on Deli Spoorweg Maatschappij in Sumatra.

No 2 demonstrated. The Australian cars, all of 3ft 6in gauge, were delivered in three batches, and were of slightly different types. Some of them survive today, albeit as coaches or trailers. They were numbered SP1 – SP9 and were delivered as body shells, boilers and running gear. They were fitted out locally.

SP1 and SP2 (works Nos. 8410-1 of 1931) were coal-fired cars, 9 feet wide and 57 feet long. They had one engine and a vertical boiler. First- and second-class saloons were further divided into smoking and non-smoking sections. Not surprisingly, the first class section was furthest from the driving end! These cars were used at first on evening services between Hobart and Launceston, a distance of 133 miles, but they were soon transferred to the Western line. After the newer cars had been introduced, in May 1940 SP1 was used between Burnie and Smithton (53 miles) and SP2 between Launceston and St Mary's (82 miles). Both cars were serviced in 1944, but their use dwindled and they were put into store in 1949. At this time their steam apparatus was removed and they re-entered service in 1950 as passenger cars. In this form they were used on various services until going to the Van Diemen Light Railway Society (VDRS). Unfortunately, they were both scrapped in the 1980s.

SP3 and SP4 (works Nos. 8811-2 of 1933) were similar to the first two cars, but were slightly longer and had both bogies powered; the leading, or boiler-end, bogie had six wheels. They had a horizontal, Woolnough boiler. Because of their extra power, they were well able to tow a trailer. Consequently, they may have been provided with a corridor connection (really just a door, rather like that to be found on London Underground stock) at the non-boiler or No 2 end. (Pictures show this feature on SP3, but not until after it was de-engined). They took over the service on the line between Launceston and Hobart and ran with trailers on boat train services. Later they were used on a variety of services, but by 1949 SP3 ran under its own steam for the last time. SP4 soldiered on until August 1950, but was said to be unreliable. They were both converted to coach use and lasted in very occasional service until 1977. SP3 was scrapped in 1980, but SP4 went to the Tasmanian Transport Museum. In 1999 it was fully and splendidly restored (though as a non-powered coach) and is in now use on special trains. The museum's website (www.railtasmania.com) has wonderful pictures of this car.

The now scrapped SP1 (de-engined) at Hobart in November 1974. It is coupled to a later car (Darryl Grant).

SP5 or SP8 at the Bellarine Peninsula Ralway, Queenscliffe station in 1989 (Darryl Grant)

Five more cars, SP5 – SP9 (works Nos. 9201- 2, 9234-5, 9238 of 1937), entered service in 1937. They were in many ways similar to SP3 and 4, but they were oil-fired. They had 24 second class seats and 22 first; the first class section had a lavatory. There was a corridor connection at the non-boiler end. Like most Sentinels (but not perhaps some of the earlier Tasmanian cars) they could be driven from either end, but, as there was no corridor connection at the boiler end they were mostly used by being driven from that end. New diesel tanks for the fuel oil had to be provided at principal stations.

These cars were intensively used on the kind of services we have already noted. On the Oatlands branch they could be seen attached to up to three goods wagons, making them rare Sentinel mixed trains. During the war years, however, the cars were used less and less. SP6 lost its traction equipment as early as 1946 and the others were similarly treated by 1949, suggesting that they were less well-liked than the earlier cars. Their demise may in part, however, have been because of the difficulty of obtaining fuel oil during the war years.

At the same time as these cars were ordered, four steel-bodied buffet coaches were ordered from Clyde Engineering and built at Granville, New South Wales. These and the Sentinels were lined out in polished wood with blackwood framing. The ceiling was white and there were swing doors and glass partitions to separate the classes and the smoking saloons. When used with the Sentinels they were marshalled so that the corridor connections were together. Together the buffets and the Sentinels worked the "Main Line" services from Hobart to Launceston.

At one time there was a plan to rebuild the cars as diesels, but, although parts were ordered, nothing was ever done, leaving them to be used as saloons until their usefulness expired. They were all written off in 1978, but SP5 and SP8 were sent to the Bellarine Peninsula Railway (BPR – they are still there) and SP7 to the VDRS. SP9 went to the Wee Georgie Wood Preservation Project and then to a private collector at Strahan. SP6 went to the VDRS but then passed to the Tasmanian Locomotive Company at Cadbury, Claremont, in Tasmania. Later, after a series of moves which included the removal of its interior, it was bought by Mr. Michael Wood and fitted out as a Pullman restaurant car.

The liveries carried by Tasmanian Sentinels varied a lot. At first they seem to have been turned out in dark red, but SP1 and 2 were painted red and cream when de-engined. SP3 and 4 were also dark red when running under their own power, but SP3 was given cherry red and SP4 green later. The biggest surprise is the original livery of the oil-fired cars, which defies description. They were cream with swirling emerald green designs on the sides and ends. They had green roofs and red buffer beams. They must have been quite a sight!

N.W.State Rly India, Kangra Valley Section

The Kangra railway, 2ft 6 in gauge, linking Pathankot and Joginder Nagar (originally in connection with a power station project) gently meanders through a maze of hills and valleys, offering the travellers enchantingly scenic views. The work on this line started in 1926. In 1928 this 163 km long route was opened to traffic. Three years after that, in 1932, Sentinel delivered works Nos. 8470-2. These were single cars (they are illustrated in the catalogue), and were almost certainly of the 200 – 300 hp design. They had luxurious interiors, with both first- and second-class saloons having leather 2+1 seating. They were NWR class ZZTL, numbered 2 – 4. The Kangra Valley Railway is today a major tourist attraction in the region and is to remain narrow gauge, but no trace of the Sentinels has yet been found.

Nyasaland Railways

"The Sentinel steam rail-cars, of 120-125 horse-power, were introduced into Nyasaland in 1933 for Hindoos and Africans. Since the fares on the rail-car are lower than those on ordinary trains, the natives have been induced to travel more frequently, and labour is becoming rather more fluid in the Protectorate. It has also been possible to reduce the number of mixed trains which carried passengers and goods now that the natives use the rail-cars." This amazing statement is from a report to the railway management and refers to works Nos. 8689-90 of 1931 for the 3ft 6inch gauge railway. They were numbered SR1 and SR2. The information which follows has been provided by Ray Ellis.

In common with a number of railways throughout the world at the time, in 1932 the NR purchased two steam railcars for short and light local passenger runs. These cars were a joint building effort with the locomotive part built by Sentinel and the body work by the Metropolitan Carriage, Wagon & Finance Co. They were classified SC and numbered 1 and 2, though at some later stage of their careers they were reclassified SRC. They seem to have been successful on the NR and continued in active service until withdrawal in February 1963 when they were relegated to the Limbe scrap road where they languished for many years. They suffered a better fate than many of their counterparts around the world. Generally steam railcars tended to have their engine units removed and ended up as carriages when the traffic became too great for them to handle. This did not happen to these cars, and they continued to be used as SRCs to the end. Because these NR cars were still 'complete', British railway enthusiasts expressed some interest in the preservation of one of the units, but nothing eventuated, probably because of the high cost of shipment and restoration, and both were eventually scrapped.

NYASALAND RAILWAYS LTD. - Timetables for Steam Railmotors

WTT No. 7 effective from 5th February 1940

Down

Train No.	Calculated from Dondo Junction	11		13		15	
Type		SRC		SRC		SRC	
Day		Tuesdays & Fridays		Mondays		Saturdays	
Station	Mileage	arr	dep	arr	dep	arr	dep
Balaka	399	No Service Shown		No Service Shown		No Service Shown	
Limbe	330		0915		1110		
Blantyre	335	0935	'0945	1130	1140		
Limbe	330	1006	1016	1201	1210		
Luchenza	302	1200	1210	1353			
Chiromo	253						1600
Port Herald	222	1651				1712	

Up

Train No.	6		8		10		12	
Type	SRC		SRC		SRC		SRC	
Day	Sundays		Wednesdays		Saturdays		Mondays	
Station	arr	dep	arr	dep	arr	dep	arr	dep
Port Herald		1025		1035		1215		
Chiromo	1136	1146	1146	1156	1327			
Luchenza	1519	1529	1537	1547				1400
Limbe	1721	1730	1739	1749			1552	1600
Blantyre	1750	1800	1809	1819			1620	1630
Limbe	1821		1840				1651	
Balaka	No Service Shown		No Service Shown		No Service Shown		No Service Shown	

NOTE: There are no Steam Railcars timetabled north of Blantyre in this WTT (although other trains are shown ok)

Ammendment to WTT No. 7 for Monday 2nd April to Wednesday 4th April

Down

Train No.	18		10		20		6	
Type	SRC		SRC		SRC		SRC	
Day	Monday 2nd April		Monday 2nd April		Tuesday 3rd April		Wednesday 4th April	
Station	arr	dep	arr	dep	arr	dep	arr	dep
Limbe		1000		1500		0850		1445
Blantyre	1020		1525		0910		1505	

Up

Train No.	15		21		11		19	
Type	SRC		SRC		SRC		SRC	
Day	Monday 2nd April		Monday 2nd April		Tuesday 3rd April		Wednesday 4th April	
Station	arr	dep	arr	dep	arr	dep	arr	dep
Blantyre		1031		1535		0920		1515
Limbe	1052		1556		0941		1536	

WTT No. 12 effective from 2nd April 1945

Down

Train No.	209		11		15		17	
Type	SRC		SRC		SRC		SRC	
Day	Sun / Mon / Tues		Tuesdays & Fridays		Mondays		Saturdays	
Station	arr	dep	arr	dep	arr	dep	arr	dep
Balaka		1140						
Blantyre	1522							
Limbe				0950		1100		
Luchenza			1140	1148	1245			
Chiromo			1507	1512				1450
Port Herald			1645				1610	

Up

Train No.	206		208		?		?		14	
Type	SRC		SRC		SRC		SRC		SRC	
Day	Mondays & Tuesdays		Saturdays		Wednesdays & Sundays		Mondays		Saturdays	
Station	arr	dep	arr	dep	arr	dep	arr	dep	arr	dep
Port Herald						0715				1300
Chiromo					0828	0833			1416	
Luchenza					1200	1232		1300		
Limbe					1437		1456			
Blantyre		0800		1340						
Balaka	1124		1737							

Down

Train No.	19		20		15		21		209		11		209		19		11	
Type	SRC		SRC		SRC		SRC		SRC		SRC		SRC		SRC		SRC	
Day	Sundays		Sundays		Mondays		Mondays		Mondays		Tuesdays		Tuesdays		Wednesdays		Fridays	
Station	arr	dep	arr	dep	arr	dep	arr	dep	arr	dep	arr	dep	arr	dep	arr	dep	arr	dep
Blantyre		1515		1605		1031		1535		1605		0920		1605		1515		0920
Limbe	1636		1626		1052		1556		1626		0941		1626		1536		0941	

Up

Train No.	6		206		18		10		206		20		6		20		208	
Type	SRC		SRC		SRC		SRC		SRC		SRC		SRC		SRC		SRC	
Day	Sundays		Mondays		Mondays		Mondays		Tuesdays		Tuesdays		Wednesdays		Fridays		Saturdays	
Station	arr	dep	arr	dep	arr	dep	arr	dep	arr	dep	arr	dep	arr	dep	arr	dep	arr	dep
Limbe		1445		0730		1000		1505		0730		0850		1445		0850		1310
Blantyre	1505		0750		1020		1525		0750		0910		1505		0910		1330	

Nyasaland Railway 1940 timetable

Intermediate passenger train services were also provided - between Limbe-Blantyre and Balaka, and between Blantyre-Limbe and Sena or Port Herald, either on a daily basis, or two or three days a week. Similar services were also instituted on the TZR between Sena-Inhaminga-Dondo. It was for these light intermediate services that the NR purchased the two Sentinel steam railcars. Initially these ran on the Southern Line - Limbe - Blantyre – Limbe and as far south as Port Herald, with some shorter runs, but after the opening of the Northern Extension line, they were extended to run Limbe - Balaka - Limbe. Operating daily, they handled the 120 mile round trip in about four hours in each direction, with a layover in Balaka of about an hour. On the odd occasions that both the steam railcars were out of service together, they were replaced by a locomotive hauled train of two coaches. When such an occasion occurred in 1936, interestingly the service was worked by the ex Rhodesian 7th class 4-8-0. *(from an as-yet unpublished history of Nyasaland Railways by Ray Ellis).*

The extract from the Sentinel Steam Railcars (SRC) sections of the Working Timetables (WTT) for the years 1940 and 1945 when the railway was probably at its busiest (as were many British African railways at this time) shows only the SRC timings; these are shown in the 24 hour clock for convenience, although the Working Timetables show a.m. and p.m. as the railway used at this time.

These timetables are bi-lingual (Portuguese and English) as they were also used on the Portuguese East Africa / Mozambique section as the NR / CAR and TZR were all operated as one system.

Some time after the war the running of the SRCs south of Limbe ceased, and they were concentrated on the North Line to Balaka (the service south was covered by mixed trains). This may be because they were by then starting to show their age, with no chance of replacement.

Ron Robertson, the Loco Shed Foreman at Limbe, was one of Ray's correspondents: "He more or less retired when steam ended. He was a great guy, never lost his broad Scottish accent, and retired happily to Scotland. Sadly he did not last long, and passed away after a few years. Ron loved steam, and I think the SRCs were so successful on NR due to him. He was prepared to tinker around with them and keep them in good condition and running as they should. He did, however, like the "new" diesels (the "Shire" class) and the DRCs they got, much cleaner to operate he said!"

The NR was privately owned by Nyasaland Railways Ltd. (later Malawi Railways Ltd) – a British company - and was the last British privately owned railway in all of Africa, and one of the last in the world. It probably was not a big money earner, and it suffered from all the usual criticisms about "colonial railways," but it survived and provided the locals with a reasonable service. Today it is operated under contract to the Malawi Govt. by one of the private rail operators.

Nyasaland SRC 2 - Nyasaland Railways official photo

The remains of SRC 1 at Limbe workshops, probably in 1971.

Sao Paulo Railway, Brazil

The metre-gauge EF Bragantina was opened in 1884, running from Campo Limpo, on the (1.6 metre gauge) Sao Paulo Railway, to Braganza. In 1903 it was purchased by the SPR. In 1913, it was extended to Bandeirantes (Vargas), on the border with Minas Gerais, and in 1914, to Piracaia. It was closed and lifted in 1967.

Sentinel works No. 8813 was bought for this line in 1933. It is recorded in the works list as having compound cylinders, and is the only narrow-gauge railmotor shown in this way; it may have been broad gauge as Abbott's list shows a broad gauge railcar for San Paulo Railway itself.

Initially it was used for passenger service, and later as an ambulance.

IV Centenario, possibly the dieselised 8813. (Courtesy of Kelso Médici with thanks to Antonio Augusto Gorni)

JOURNEYS BY SENTINEL

What follows attempts to put together five journeys by Sentinel-Cammell railcar. Some of the detail is guesswork, but the writing is based on various pieces of evidence which have come to light during the research for this book. The title of each piece includes reference to its (often sketchy) origins.

The exception to the above is the fifth piece, the Sri Lankan journey, which I have placed last, even though that disturbs the order dictated by the rest of the book. This journey is the recollection of Les Nixon, and is the only first-hand memory by someone who actually travelled on one of the cars that I have come across so far.

A Holidaymaker in Jersey
(a fictitious account based on anecdote and inference!)

Let us mingle with the crowd at St. Helier on a warm day in June 1931. Ahead of us is the impressive station building and, with a few other holidaymakers, we are going to ride out to First Tower to get a good look at St. Aubin's Bay and to get away from the hurly-burly of the town.

We buy a first class ticket and drift on to the platform, where, waiting in the station is *The Pioneer No. 1*. We notice that it is standing on the traverser which was put in to allow locomotives to run around their trains in double quick time. No such need for the railmotor! The rear end of the car looks like a typical product of Sentinel-Cammell with its bowed windows, head and tail light and the name painted in an arc. The green and yellow colour scheme reminds us of the island buses, as indeed it should since it is evidence of common ownership.

Most holidaymakers are heading for second class, but we have a little further to walk. We can post those cards we've just written in the box between second and first, and then we reach the door to First Class. This gives us a bit of trouble until we realise that it opens inwards in defiance of convention. To our right is the tractor unit and we cannot resist a peep through the connection to this. There in front of us is the water tank and beyond that the footplate where stand driver and mate. The boiler is set a little to the left so that it can be fired whilst the driver stands to the controls at the right.

No doubt, many will sneer at all this. Those who, calling themselves railway enthusiasts, enjoy watching and listening to the products of Eastleigh or Swindon Works will find little that is familiar here. The cylinders drive the wheels through a chain! But the secrets of the vehicle's success are that high-pressure boiler and that valve gear, secrets that have made the name of Sentinel the mark of top quality in steam road motors. Here there is no highly polished dome or pipe work; here no complicated superheater or hungry firebox, but a simple vertical boiler whose funnel goes out through the roof of what would otherwise be a passenger carriage. The driver is as close to his machinery as it is possible to be, but he has a view of the line ahead that many a top link man would envy.

Reluctantly, we turn to our left and find ourselves in an oasis of calm. There are twelve seats, and the middle four have reversible backs so that we settle ourselves in them facing in the forward direction. Surely it is time to depart? We glance behind us to the Second Class and find that ten or twelve people are in the commodious saloon. They have the same large windows with opening hoppers as we do, the same view and the same schedule, but unlike us, they have some grizzling

The Pioneer from an early postcard

children and one or two contentious parents to entertain them. Their seats are rather harder than ours, too. We have the comparative luxury of padded royal-blue seats, but they must make do with a yellowish cloth and wooden supports. They can, however, read the various announcements and advertisements provided for their information: they are not permitted to spit and they should visit Mr DeGrouchy's Drapery. We, on the other hand, appear to be able to do exactly as we please.

But what is that noise? We strain to look through to the footplate and, yes, the fireman is carefully placing some small nuggets of coal on the glowing ring of fire in the small firebox. Meanwhile, our driver leans out of the curious duckett provided for him and acknowledges the green flag. A groan such as might be given by an overloaded wooden platform is followed by a distinct puff and a clank. The chain, the cylinders and the wheels are all taking the strain. Let's not try to talk, as these noises, multiplied by ten, are repeated every moment until we perceive that we are crawling away from the station. On our left, the bay begins to appear, and on our right, the station fence gives way to the seafront road backed by buildings: houses, shops and small businesses.

Our speed must now be at least fifteen miles an hour and the temperature of the saloon has risen perhaps by the same number of degrees. And is that stray smoke that is making its way towards us? The seat back, which had seemed so easy to adjust is now shaking as if a palsy had infected it. The outward opening window hoppers look fair to break their glasses. The noise of the recalcitrant children is now quite gone. We are well under way.

A hiss of steam informs us that the brake has been applied. Thoughts that some emergency might be overtaking us are dismissed as the first stop appears to our right. This is Bellozanne Halt, just under half a mile from the terminus. It may well be the most renamed station in the world, as it opened as Cheapside in 1872, was quickly renamed Westmount but became West Park in 1896. In 1872 a popular fervour titled it People's Park until it gained its present name as recently as 1923! We stop. The blessed silence is welcome, but the heat and the smoke remain. Surely this should be third, or perhaps sixth class.

As we restart, the sounds we heard before are repeated. The views of the bay to our left are truly breathtaking, but our breath has already been taken. There is but one thing to do; reluctantly, we stand and, holding tight to the seat backs, open the connecting door to the second class and pass through. The noise of the children is but a pleasant burble compared to what we have just left, and the arguing adults are really quite amusing. The air is clear and relatively pure and we are pulling in to First Tower. It is quite a walk through the whole of second class to the door, but we do not intend to return the way we have come so we lurch to the back of the vehicle and step out on to the platform. A green flag, a toot on the whistle (we couldn't hear that from inside) and *The Pioneer No.1* pulls away and we are left to the sounds of the sea. We shall walk back to St. Helier, I think.

After a Day's Work in New Zealand
(another journey based on snippets from the past)

In 1926, after a day's business in Auckland, I caught the Auckland to Wellington express and am returning to my home in Thames. We left Auckland at 7.45 and arrived at Frankton Junction at 10.24. It's been a full day and a number of people are waiting at Frankton Junction to catch the 10.35 branch train. Never having been so late back before, I am surprised at the train which is waiting for us. Here is a maroon articulated coach with doors at each end of the larger section and a wide bank of windows along the side. There are curtains at the windows and the far end of the coach, the smaller part, has similar windows. Out of the foremost of these leans a uniformed figure who must be the driver. A wisp of steam escapes from a funnel at the very front of the roof.

There are about twenty of us waiting for permission to board, and here comes the guard. He directs us to the front doors, opens them and, smiling, ushers us in to the comfortable saloon. The seats are covered in leather and are reversible like those of a tramcar. Between us and the driving section is a light screen which will no doubt protect us from the smells of the engine and a luggage rack of woven string runs down either side of the roof. The car is provided with electric lights and, given

Rm1 at Lambton (Wellington) 1925. (NZ Model Railway Journal)

the time of night, these are illuminated so that we can find our places with ease. Indeed, it would be quite possible to read a book if we had one with us.

At the rear doors, railwaymen are loading parcels of newspaper for offloading at our various stops and at Thames itself. The carriage has no real luggage space, so these papers are occupying the short section to the rear of the doors, where there is a driving position should it be necessary to operate the car in the other direction.

After a look around, the passengers dispose themselves around the carriage. No one sits too close to anyone else. Indeed, some look as if they are settling themselves for a nap, and others bury themselves in newspapers, magazines and books. As it is a warm evening, a good number of the inward-opening hopper windows are letting in some air. The guard checks our tickets and, bang on 10.35, shuts the folding doors at the front. He walks to the back doors and holds out the green flag. The result is a piercing whistle as he closes this door too. He takes a seat immediately.

Movement is slight at first, but the clanking soon becomes quite loud; no doubt the chain drive is to blame. The six minutes to our first stop at Hamilton is spent in getting used to the very unusual motion, more like that of a horse-drawn cart than of a train, though rather faster, of course. At Hamilton, six more hopefuls join us, finding seats and settling after showing their tickets. The guard's performance at the back door is repeated.

As we speed down the track (it seems very fast indeed) we let out that piercing whistle at regular intervals as we pass over the many road crossings on the line. As it is impossible to see the countryside, I concentrate on the scene inside the car. Everyone is in movement: that man with the hat is gently shaking from side to side, and the couple with three baskets are trying to prevent them from falling of the seat beside them. Having put my own briefcase on the rack, I constantly check to see that it is staying put. Perhaps the motion has lulled that large man into an early sleep, as what seems to be a snore has just come from his direction.

And then we stop again. Stopping is something of an adventure. First the hiss of the steam brake, then the roar of brake block on wheel, then the juddering and slowing and finally the screech as metal brings metal to a halt. Each time I wonder if it will be easier now that the driver is into his stride, and each time it is not.

Official timetables show a possible twenty-four stops, but we flash through a good number of small places where only a name board shows that a stop is possible. However, at Morrinsville, Waitoa, Te Aroha and Paeroa we stop and unload some of those papers, but twice, we stop at what seems to be just a road crossing to let people off. Peering through the window reveals just a ghost of the flat meadow land through which we are passing. On the outskirts of Te Aroha, we rumble over the Waihu River bridge and soon we are screeching to a halt again. The principal stations on this line are wooden frame buildings with a canopy stretching over the platform.

By the time we get to Waitoki, we are running alongside the main road to Paeroa, and it is here that two more people get out. There is no sign of house or habitation! After more newspaper unloading at Paeroa, we continue to run through the Hauraki Plains, through Hikutaia to Thames. Home at last: it is 2.15am and we want our beds. Sleep has been impossible, prevented by a combination of stops, whistles and rumbling river bridges. As I thank the guard (if thank is the word!), he tells me that in an hour's time he begins the return trip. He'll be back at Frankton by 6.30 in the morning. Now he must help turn the carriage.

Fish from New Harbor in Newfoundland
(an account based around the 1928 timetable published by the company)

On Monday, Thursday and Saturday, train No. 16 goes through New Harbor at 7.52 am. It is the morning departure from Heart's Content, via Heart's Desire, Heart's Delight and Islington, and it connects at Whitbourne, twelve miles away, with train No. 2, the Express from Port-aux-Basques which arrives at St John's at noon. This makes it the perfect service to carry fish for the afternoon market.

New Harbor is a centre of shipbuilding and fishing, and until the arrival of the railway had to rely on local sales for its catch. Now, however, boxes of fish may be consigned to the railway and better prices are commanded. Put on carts, they are wheeled to the station early in the morning, having been packed in ice the previous day.

A small group of fishermen waits on the platform. This is not a "flag" station so they expect the train to stop. Today (and every day) the train consists of Sentinel Unit D, which has plenty of space for the fish. Just along the platform the mail man waits; he will exchange his few letters and parcels for inward bound ones when the train arrives (though more mail will arrive by train No. 15 at 1.20 p.m.).

The train can be heard before it is seen; the strange panting of the six-cylinder engine is familiar to all who wait and the plume of smoke from the spark-arrester is the first indication of its position. It is often late; after all, the timetable is clear: "It is not guaranteed that the starting time or the arriving time of trains shall be as published herein, neither will this Railway be liable for loss or damage arising from delays or detentions." In this society, a little time lost is neither here nor there.

As the car crosses the dirt road at the end of the station, the passenger section passes the men first. As usual, there is a handful of people on board. Many of the travellers are in some way connected with the transatlantic cable station at Heart's Content, where messages from Britain have arrived on the American continent since the *Great Eastern* completed the laying of two cables in 1886. (Having laid the second successfully she and her consorts then went back to find the end of the first broken cable, lift it, repair it and complete the laying of it!)

The guard leaps from the car and opens his great sliding door so that the fish and the mails may be loaded. The mail goes into the special compartment closest to the boiler (in this case the trailing) end, and the fish into the section between the mail and the passengers, no doubt adding to the aroma in the second class on the remaining 53 minutes which it will take the car to make the twelve mile journey to Whitbourne.

Little did they know it, but the branch was to close in 1931.

At a station in Newfoundland. (1929 catalogue).

Alice rides the Bombay, Baroda and Central India
(a fictional account)

The station at Indore is an enormous cavern which echoes to the sound of whistles, doors slamming, people shouting and the ever present movement of trains to and from Bombay. Having arrived in the relative comfort of a fast train she looks round for some help with her two battered suitcases.

"Porter, memsahib?"

"Thank you."

"Which train?"

"I'm going to Mhow."

The eyebrows rise as if Mhow is an impossible dream, but, "Follow" and they're off up the steps to cross the line.

In a relatively quiet corner of the station waits her little train: two coaches painted a dull green. A man in railway uniform lounges near the front talking through a window to another. From the roof above their heads comes a wisp of steam. As she approaches they recognise a lady and the guard, for it is he, straightens up and tries to smile.

"Luggage for the lady," calls the porter, and the door to the compartment behind where they were talking is opened and the cases carefully inserted.

"My lady, you get in here - this section is for ladies only," and she is beckoned to get in the same door as her luggage. Inside it is immensely hot and is a wide open space, but she is steered through a gangway door and finds herself in a compartment with seats along the walls and up the middle. There is no-one else there and no way out save through the guard's compartment.

What Alice missed: First class on the BB&CI (with the Driver's compartment beyond). (1929 catalogue.)

"When do we leave?" she asks, only to be met with a shrug. They should have gone already, but they are waiting for a connection from Vadorada. It's late. It's always late, but there is a good chance it'll come within the hour. He closes the communicating door and she is left to her thoughts. From her bag she takes the letter which has brought her here. It is creased with much reading, but she goes over it all once again. Mhow is the headquarters of the 5th (Mhow) Division of the Southern Army. The British Signal Training Centre there (STC(B)) is officered by graduates from Catterick Camp and her husband has decided that she should join him, although this is very unusual. He'll certainly be waiting for her when she arrives, he says, and she reflects that that will mean a long wait for him now, as it seems they won't be leaving until they should have arrived! For a long time she lets her thoughts go where they will; waiting in patience is something she's fast learning in this extraordinary land.

At last there is more shouting and slamming of doors. The only way to see out is to kneel upon the seat, raise the shade and press ones nose on the glass. She carries out this manoeuvre only to see raised eyebrows from the guard. Clearly it is not a ladylike thing to do. There are people getting into her train further back, but no-one makes for the ladies' section. And yet, surely, some of them are women. Perhaps they cannot afford first class travel. She decides that she would rather be back there with others, but when she knocks on the door and asks the guard he is scandalised. "You lady, cannot mix with them," waves his hand and gets in to the train. Resigned to her loneliness, she settles on the seat again as a piercing whistle from just ahead of her announces their departure.

There is a strange sucking sound from under the floor as the train starts to move and then a sussuration which continues throughout the journey. It is very hot.

There are shanties both sides of the track now and the poverty she has seen elsewhere is close at hand. Children in rags wave at the train, some even jumping up and clinging on for a few moments until dropping away again with a cackle of laughter. Gradually fields replace the squalor and flat land stretches away as far as she can see.

Soon the shanties start again and the station at Rau is reached. Most people seem to get off here, and certainly no one enters her private world. Again the doors slamming and the whistles, again the sucking sound and swishing and they're off. This time there is more of a break between the shanties of Rau and those of Mhow, as the fields stretch away into the distance.

This time when the brakes squeal and the train draws to a halt, it is Mhow that she sees written on the name board. Eagerly she presses her face to the window; is he there? Could that be him at the other end of the train? Emboldened by arrival, she opens the door and steps into the stiflingly hot guard's van. The platform door presents itself, so out she hops. It is him! She waves and he rushes up to her.

"Surely, you didn't come from in there?"

"Yes, it's for ladies."

"It's for women. Women who need to be kept separate from men. British ladies travel first class." She giggles. It's going to be all right.

A Sri Lankan Interlude
(recollections of Les Nixon)

During the period September 1973 to January 1975 I was resident in Sri Lanka and came to know the railways in some detail. At the time I was delighted to be able to see and ride behind a fairly large selection of broad gauge steam locomotives among which the class C1A 2-6-2 + 2-6-2 Garratts were undoubtedly the highlight. A climb through exotic tea country to a summit at Pattipola (6226ft. above sea level) was an experience never to be forgotten.

On the narrow gauge though, there were disappointments, but one surviving highlight; the KVR (Kelani Valley Railway). Sadly the branch line from Avissawella to Yattiyantota and the Up Country line (UPR) from Nanu Oya through Nuwara Eliya to Ragalla had both closed soon after the outbreak of WW2.

The 2ft 6in gauge KV line ran from Colombo to Avissawella, on to Ratnapura and then to a terminus at Opanayake. Latterly steam motive power was primarily the Class J1 and J2 4-6-4 tanks built by Hunslet and North British between 1909 and 1928. The jewel in the crown though was undoubtedly the three steam railcars. Built by Sentinel (works no 7303-5) in 1928 and classified V2 they were numbered 331-3.

In 1973 they shared duties from Ratnapura to Opanayake with the class P1 and N2 diesels. The latter usually worked two coaches which provided pro rata more space than the single car V2 and this, coupled with the fact that the ride was somewhat quieter than the railcars, meant that they were marginally the preferred option for the travelling public.

Apart from trips on the regular services down the branch my most abiding memory of the railcars was a return trip through the night on 15 March 1974. My good friend Ken Plant and I had arrived at Ratnapura only to be disappointed that a diesel had been diagrammed for the day's services. However just outside the small running shed opposite the single platform station No. 332 was being serviced by a small group of fitters and more importantly we learned it was being steamed for trials a little later in the day. In the event departure was well after dark at about 19.00 and we were invited to join the trip. We didn't need a second invitation even though we had no idea of what the return time might be – certainly we were told it could be in the wee small hours of the morning!

I vividly recall two fitters working in the semi darkness on the cylinders and transmission through trap doors in the floor. On the move it was very noisy, very hot and humid and certainly not a particularly smooth ride. However the guys with the spanners seemed to make various adjustments (with the help of a sizeable hammer at times) although it all seemed to be rather a trial and error exercise. The run through the tropical night was quite magical with 'jungly noises' and at times sparks flying high out of the chimney. Stops for more serious adjustments were sometimes made in the middle of the jungle and Sri Lankan refreshments were on offer at the intermediate station of Dela – but we cared little – THIS was an experience of a life time. We arrived exhausted back at Ratnapura at 01.00 when we then checked into our reserved basic accommodation at the Government Rest House overlooking the station. Truly it was a night to remember.

Some weeks later I returned to Ratnapura when the same railcar was in service and the driver immediately recognised me. This was a photographic rather than a riding visit and when I requested 'coal on the fire for smoke at certain locations please' (to ensure the train looked like a steam rather than a diesel car) he smiled broadly... He had worked with the British for many years and knew of their humour and their liking for tea. He paused, looked at the small pile of coal by the vertical boiler and replied... "certainly Sir - one lump or two!"

A good view of the guard's compartment of Ceylon Railways No. 331. (Robin Patrick)

Sadly today the line has been long closed beyond Ratnapura (1976) and Avissawella (1978). Further, the surviving remnant has suffered the indignity of conversion to the island's broad gauge but it does now provide a much improved commuter service to the capital, Colombo.

A recent visit to the running shed at Dematagoda in Colombo revealed a very short stretch of surviving narrow gauge track along with a number of mainly complete J1 and J2 tanks plus V2 railcar No. 331. The latter was apparently in working order and in relatively good condition, but sadly with nowhere to go it is little more than a static exhibit

Perhaps in the long term a short preserved narrow gauge line might be reconstructed, perhaps out of the Up Country resort of Nuwara Eliya on the old UPR (Uda Pussalawa Railway), but in the present economic climate of Sri Lanka it seems highly unlikely. One thing is certain though - it would be a huge tourist attraction.

APPENDIX 1: CATALOGUES

Sentinel were intensely publicity conscious and their catalogues were full of what would today be called "hard-sell". The main text of this history refers to this from time to time, but the determined Sentinel enthusiast needs more: there is space here for only a brief review, however. So far, six catalogues which refer to the railcars have come to light.

Sentinel Rail Coach Catalogue 1922

We know that the first railcar *The Pioneer* was produced in June 1923, but a catalogue dated 1/5/22 is given the title *R2*, suggesting that there may have been an even earlier attempt to sell to the rail industry. This catalogue (along with the 1929 and 1931 editions, seen courtesy of the J.L. Thomas collection with thanks to Tony Thomas) not surprisingly contains no photos of railcars or locos, since no vehicles had yet been produced. Catalogue R1 may have included locomotives, but this edition is exclusively for "rail coaches". Absence of vehicles does not prevent the presentation of "facts":

This booklet tells of:- 1. Motor Railway Coaches, the traffic which they create, and the large profits which they earn. 2. The "Sentinel" Rail Coach, the details of its construction, operation, running costs, prices, etc. 3. Its profit-making uses to Railways, the World over. 4. Ourselves and the "Sentinel" Waggon Works.

There are drawings of a number of variations of a four-wheel car which can seat about 33 people. If used for journeys of 150 miles a day, it will make the operator a (annual?) profit of £2,261, but if paired with a trailer £3,277 may be expected. There are many more such figures quoted.

It is interesting that nowhere in this work of fiction does the name "Cammell" appear, but much is made of 18 years of experience building steam waggons. Obviously, this lends the catalogue an air of authority:

The Uses for Railway Motor Coaches

Railways lose much valuable traffic because of their difficulty in economically moving small numbers of passengers or small lots of goods with the rolling stock hitherto available.

Railway Managers have now at their disposal the smaller steam-driven units illustrated in this booklet, and instead of having to use expensive trains at a loss, or being reluctantly driven to leaving the smaller, more frequent traffic alone or at the disposal of competing road motor transport, can carry 33 passengers at a cost below four pence per train mile, or 66 passengers at a train mile cost of five pence.

By this means alone can road motor competition be successfully met, and the large potential minor traffic of any area be fully converted to profit.

These are not mere statements, for earlier trials with coaches much more costly to buy and operate have shown surprising results in handling minor traffic profitably, which results stand to be greatly increased by the more economical service possible with " Sentinel " Coaches.

Railway Managers comparing the costs with the revenue obtainable even where the coaches have to be run half empty, as is allowed for in the figures printed opposite, which are fully detailed on pages 11 to 13, will find this a matter for complete investigation, and to this end we hold ourselves willingly at their disposal.

This confidence is found later in the catalogue when many types of rail coach, narrow-, metre- and broad- gauge have been examined along with their (theoretical) running costs and advantages:

Petrol Driven Coaches.

We have also examined a number of designs of these, but while they have the advantage of light weight, it does not seem that they should be taken seriously into consideration. Explosion engines must of course be used with all their disadvantages of high temperatures and much higher speeds, which are not conducive to long life. Then they require a clutch and that rather barbarous change speed gear, also a reduction to the driving axle. They have also the possibility of electrical and carburation troubles, which are out of place on a railway. If the engine is compared with the "Sentinel" Steam Engine running at 240 r.p.m — less than one-third of the speed, and therefore subjected to less than one-ninth of the inertia stresses — operated by non-explosive steam impulses without change speed gear, able to smoothly increase its tractive effort to 2,800 lbs. by infinitely small increments, without shock to the passengers or its own mechanism, and easily understood by railway men, these points alone, without the large economy in running expenses, are sufficient to decide the matter.

Reliability.

Great as are the savings by the use of "Sentinel" Steam Road Waggons, users have told us that it is not the economy alone which makes them order from us, it is also the lower upkeep costs, and the much greater reliability. They know when they send out a "Sentinel" they may cease to think of it until it comes back at its appointed hour; they have no fear of breakdowns, for the whole machine is so simple and strong that there is practically nothing to get out of order.

How could the customer resist?

The catalogue details the Sentinel boiler and cylinders by using photographs of road waggon equipment and goes on to describe the running gear and bodywork of the coaches. Presumably, this was the result of development work:

The Body Frames, which are bolted to the steel underframes, and to which are attached the floor, sides, roof, and ends, are of oak or other seasoned hardwood, the roof beams being of ash. The members of these frames are firmly secured to each other at the corners by bolts through steel plate brackets, one on either side of each member, and are amply rigid to stand any usual stresses or shocks.

An ample supply of brass screws and steel bolts is sent with each coach or trailer coach. (!)

No such coaches were ever built.

"Sentinel-Cammell" Steam Rail Coaches – issued 1925

What happened between the 1922 catalogue outlined above and this edition is not clear. As Sentinel literature is so difficult to trace, it may be that someone has some intervening literature which throws light on the abandonment of the "go-it-alone" spirit and the connection with Cammell-Laird.

The 1925 catalogue (which along with the 1927 edition we have courtesy of Ray Ellis) still speaks of Rail Coaches, but the introduction, fulsome as ever, comments:

The Coaches are the joint production of Messrs. The "Sentinel" Waggon Works, Ltd., of Shrewsbury, who manufacture and supply the Power Units, and of Messrs. Cammell Laird & Co., Ltd., Nottingham, who are responsible for the general design, manufacture and erection of the vehicles as a whole.

There can be little doubt that the same hands prepared this catalogue, since it continues to make extravagant claims as before:

Revenue Earning Capacity
Standard Single Coach, Type "A"

(56 Passengers).
Daily mileage 200
Daily seat miles 11,200
Daily earning capacity at 1½d. per seat mile *(assuming Coach run only half full)* £35
Daily working expenses at 6.13d. per train mile £5.11s.0d
Daily Nett Earnings.. £29.9s.0d
Annual Nett Earnings (300 days) £8,970

Double Articulated Coach, Type "Y"

(112 Passengers).
Daily mileage 200
Daily seat miles 22,400
Daily earning capacity at 1½d. per seat mile *(assuming Coach run only half full)* £70
Daily working expenses at 7.65d. per train mile £6.3s.0d
Daily Nett Earnings.. £63.7s.0d
Annual Nett Earnings (300 days) £20,110

56'-4"
Type "A" 56 Passengers.

42'-4"
Type "B" 32 Passengers.

96'-10"
Type "Y" 112 Passengers.

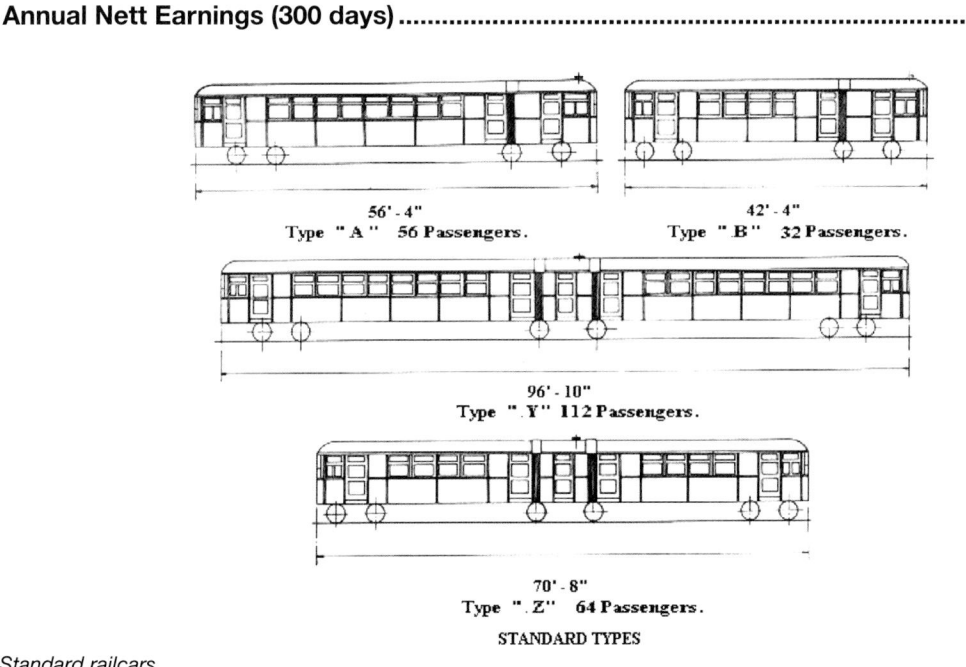

70'-8"
Type "Z" 64 Passengers.

STANDARD TYPES

Standard railcars

The above figures indicate the relatively enormous revenues to be obtained from the use of these Coaches, and justify their adoption for developing sparsely populated districts.

From this may be seen that the coaches were now being offered in a number of differing guises. In fact, four types, bizarrely named "A"; "B"; "Y" & "Z" were offered:

All of these were articulated, Type "A" being the only one that had been produced in narrow gauge form up to the time of the catalogue, though Type "Z" was delivered to the 2ft 6in gauge Bengal Nagpur (Satpura) Railway as works nos. 6104, 6126, 6127 in 1926. Were the other types ever built?

This catalogue contains many pictures of the cars (almost all Type "A") and details of the running gear, boilers and engines. The element of fantasy has not altogether departed: *The principal advantage of the "Sentinel" Engine may, therefore, be summed up as follows: Economy. Initially high and easily maintained. Durability. Unsurpassed, due principally to ample and well protected bearing surfaces. Power. Comparatively great for its size and developed over a large range of speeds. Ease of Control. Such that on late cut-off the Rail Coach can be moved by inches.* - but it is now subordinate to solid fact!

Every illustration and description is accompanied by a telegraphic code using Bentley's code, so the Bengal Nagpur (Satpura) Railway no doubt sent ZAVYN to Shrewsbury and received their units by return of post. ZAWPY would have got you the catalogue!

Interestingly, the engine described in this catalogue is of the two-cylinder vertical type and works number 6104 was the first narrow gauge example to be fitted with this expedient. The photo captions do not reveal that the pictured cars have horizontal engines, however.

When the catalogue turns its attention to the coachwork, one cannot avoid the impression that a different hand is at work. It seems altogether more practical and the details are impressive. It is worth quoting at length:

General Construction
The General Arrangement of the Power Unit is shown on page 8, and the tables on pages 27 and 29 show the varying widths, etc., for different gauges.

Engine Bogie. *The bogie carrying the Power Unit consists of an underframe on which is fixed the Engine and Boiler, Coal Bunkers, etc. At the rear end, near the car body, and practically over the rear axle, is the pivot for carrying the forward end of the car body.*

The Bogie Frame is supported on four laminated bearing springs bolted to the axle boxes.

In order to permit the adjustment of the driving chains, the axles are arranged so that their position may be varied relative to the bogie frame and to each other.

Underframe. *The underframe, as will he seen from the illustration on opposite page, is of a light but strong construction of the cantilever type, comprising two channel steel centre sills with braced crossbars carrying the Coach sides and the floor. Each crossbar has attachments at its extremities for receiving the car body pillars. The centre sills are reinforced by angle steel trussing.*

The forward end of the frame is provided with the pivot resting on the Engine Bogie. The top half of the pivot is of cast steel and rests on a special rubber spring to obviate any vibration. It is maintained in position by a steel seating anchoring the pivot in its correct relation to the underframe, but permitting it to adapt itself to the rubber cushion and to the oscillation of the car body.

The trailing end of the underframe is provided with a bolster, fitted with cast steel centre pivots and cast steel side bearers.

Coach Body Sides. The coach consists of a light steel framing with steel waist panels. The side pillars of I-section are attached at the lower end to the underframe crossbars with which they coincide. The steel waist panel is riveted to the side pillars, and is flanged at its upper and lower edges to provide the necessary stillness longitudinally.

The cantrail of the bodyside consists of a steel angle riveted to the upper ends of the body side pillars.

Cab Front and Rear End. The ends of the Coach are built up of steel pillars with steel waist panels.

Each end is provided with openings for three windows.

Doorways. Two doorways for the passengers are provided on each side of the car, arranged to provide a clear opening of 2ft 6in.

Roof. The roof framing and outer sheeting is of steel.

The roof ribs are of steel angles, on which the roof sheets of steel are lapped and riveted to provide a water-tight joint.

Engine Cab. The construction of the engine cab is identical with that of the car body. A doorway giving a clear opening of 2 ft 6in is provided on each side.

The front end of the cab is identical with that at the rear end of the car body.

Flexible Connection. The space between the Coach Body and the Cab is closed by a flexible connection and by a steel cover plate on the top between the two roofs, allowing freedom of movement on curves.

Internal Equipment. The internal equipment of "Sentinel-Cammell" Coaches is made to suit the requirements of individual customers for tropical, temperate and frigid climates. The general construction allows for the fitting of sliding windows and louvres for tropical countries, fixed windows and hinged side ventilators for temperate, and double glass frames for cold climates.

Doors. Sliding doors moving on ball-bearing runners are fitted to both Engine Cab and Coach Body, between which there is also a communicating door.

Floor. The floor consists of tongued and grooved boards 1in. thick, covered with linoleum.

Interior Lining. *The interior lining of the Coach sides and ends consists of 3-ply 1-in. thick panels in the case of coaches for temperate and cold climates. Tropical Coaches are fitted with steel panels attached to hard wood furrings screwed to the steel framing.*

Seats. *Any type of seating can be supplied to suit purchasers' requirements, due consideration being given to the question of weight. Various types and arrangements of seats already fitted, together with lavatory and luggage accommodation, etc., are shown on pages 22 to 31.*

Lighting. *The Coaches are electrically lighted by a dynamo with storage battery.*

Rear Control Compartment. *A driver's compartment containing the dual control operating mechanism is fitted if required.*

Brakegear. *The coach is provided with a powerful brake operated by a pair of Vacuum Cylinders fixed in the Underframe. These are shown in the illustration on page 38. Hand brakes are also provided at each end of the Coach.*

Heating. *Steam heating can be fitted if so desired.*

The work of Cammell-Laird was solid and dependable. This is not to deprecate Sentinel's, but it is worth remembering that a number of railcars still exist as coaching stock today, whereas the power units, with one tenuous exception, are long gone.

The catalogue ends with a short section on Sentinel locomotives, all the time emphasising that railway managers worry about increasing costs and diminishing returns, a situation which the purchase of Sentinel equipment can relieve.

"Sentinel" Patent Locomotives – issued July 1927

Unlike the previous example, and as its title suggests, this catalogue was issued to sell the locomotives. There is, however a section entitled *"Sentinel-Cammell" Steam Rail Coaches* on Pages 55 – 63 (out of a total of 72). Here, the articulated car is still advertised, as the first rigid six-cylinder cars were not produced until 1928, though development must have been taking place as this catalogue was issued. We know that Cammell-Laird had been pressing for the new development since late 1926 (see Appendix 2).

Most of the text and diagrams in these pages are the same as we see in the previous catalogue, but a testimonial is worth quoting:

The Jersey Railways and Tramways Company, which in 1923 were barely paying their way owing to bus competition on the roads, purchased three "Sentinel-Cammell" coaches. In 1925 the General Manager writes: "This year we have carried over one and a quarter million passengers, paying 7 per cent. with over 7 per cent. spent on improvements.

Extract from directors' report for 1926 :- "The three 'Sentinel-Cammell' cars have given full satisfaction during the year. Notwithstanding the strike and consequential shortage of coal these cars have enabled the Company to run a full service throughout the year, which would have been impossible with the old locomotives; so that the public, the employees of the railway, and the shareholders have all benefited from the economy due to these cars."

And you can't say fairer than that.

This catalogue was provided by Ray Ellis of Brisbane and is accompanied by a letter from the manager of the Sentinel railway department dated 19th August 1927 and addressed to J.J. Petford Esq., Government Railways, Brisbane:

We have a department especially devoted to the study of locomotive and railway problems and in asking your further consideration of the possibilities or extended use "Sentinels" on the work in which you are interested, would assure you, of our close personal attention to any enquiries you may be good enough to put to us.

"Sentinel" Gear Driven Railcars – November 1929

At last the gear-driven cars are available and they are now referred to as "railcars" rather than "rail coaches". This is also the first catalogue to feature a full-colour picture of one of the cars (albeit a standard-gauge LNER example). The drawings have all been re-drawn to show rigid vehicles, but the text is in other ways very similar to previous catalogues, including the flights of fancy:

Another type of "Sentinel-Cammell" car is the light self-propelled Sleeping Car. There are many instances, particularly in tropical countries, where an ordinary sleeping car train would certainly not pay, but where between two distant towns a " Sentinel-Cammell," fitted with sleeping cabins, would prove a very profitable source of income. A journey of two hundred miles could be accomplished at a cost which would leave a substantial margin of profit.

Notice the use of the word "would". It adds: A booklet dealing with the subject of "Sentinel-Cammell Inspection and Sleeping Cars will be forwarded upon application". Whether such a document was ever written is unknown.

A good deal of this catalogue is taken up with photos and diagrams of cars recently produced, including those of the Bombay, Baroda and Central India Railway and the Leopoldina car. After the inevitable performance tables, the description of the engine is updated:

The Engine is of a 6-cylinder horizontal single-acting type, of 6-inch bore by 7-inch stroke, arranged for working with steam at 300 lbs. per sq. inch pressure and 650° F. to 750° F. temperature.

There follow a comprehensive description and a number of excellent photos. The old brief statements about the chain-drive are replaced with detailed descriptions of the gearbox drive.

Controls

All "Sentinel-Cammell" Cars, unless otherwise ordered, are constructed with controls at both ends, which enables them to be driven in either direction with equal facility, thereby dispensing with turntables.

The Control Column is situated on the right hand side of the boiler compartment and the left hand side of the driver's compartment aft. It consists of a metal column through which run two controls, the left ~hand one working the camshaft and the right hand one the steam throttle.

These fore and aft Controls are directly coupled by means of rods running under the coach floor. The Controls are designed so that only one set can be worked at a time.

Alongside the Column is a lever which controls the air brakes, straight vacuum, automatic continuous vacuum or Westinghouse.

In addition, every car is equipped with a hand brake and in extreme emergency the engine may be used as a brake.

Five boilers are offered: the standard 100-hp for reasonable quality coal, the Bengal boiler for inferior coal, the oil-fired 100-hp boiler, the 200-hp boiler and the oil-fired 200-hp boiler. Each is described in glowing terms and there are accompanying photographs of each. (See Appendix 3)

The section about coachwork is much as before and the "other advantages" section is as one would expect by now. The last part of the catalogue is devoted to locomotives, more photographs and a list of countries where "Sentinel" products are used. There are photographs of the "Sentinel" works, but none of Cammell-Lairds. One can assume, therefore, that Cammell's were happy to leave the sales in Sentinel's hands.

"Sentinel" Patent Locomotives – issued December 1931

Although nominally a locomotive catalogue, this volume includes ten pages about the railcars. They contain a digest of the information from the catalogue outlined above, together with a number of photographs. They also contain a testimonial from none other than H.N. Gresley Esq., C.B.E. (later Sir Nigel). After tabulating costs, the following is added:

The average number of Cars at work during the year was sixty-four, and it will be seen that comparison with the Auto-trains shows a saving of £103,131.

"Sentinel-Cammell" Patent Light Railway Vehicles – issued April 1932

Following close on the heels of the previous catalogue, this monster edition of 168 pages, a copy of which is in the NGRS library, once again changes title, with the word "patent" being added and the phrase "light railway vehicles" adding a touch of class. A serious foreword by S.E. Alley, Sentinel Managing Director, himself, is entitled A National Matter and runs to twenty-three pages. He carefully explains how "Sentinel-Cammell" cars are indispensable to any railway and extols the virtues of the new Railbus (recently built for the Southern Railway) which is the vehicle most closely resembling those never-built ones in the original 1922 catalogue. Only one was built, but the catalogue also offers a never-built rail lorry based on the same design. The catalogue deals with each type of railcar separately this time, but there is little new here. The technical details of the cars are covered exhaustively, however, and further details have been given in Appendix 3.

APPENDIX 2: EXTRACTS FROM THE CAMMELL LAIRD AND CO LTD COMMITTEE MINUTE BOOK 1926 - 1928

The Sentinel Company designed and built the engines, boilers and control gear of the cars and they seem to have taken responsibility for what would today be called marketing, but Cammell Laird are an important part of the story, too. Their records are a fascinating insight into a relationship which was sometimes difficult (see the references to Mr Alley, Sentinel's Managing Director, below).

It was during the currency of the 1926-28 minute book that Sentinels changed from chain- to gear-driven transmission and the six-cylinder engine was developed. Production of the Sentinel-Cammell bodywork was done at the Nottingham factory at this time, but Nottingham would be closed down in 1931 and the production moved to Saltley, Birmingham. As we see here, things were not always straightforward in the relationship between Sentinels and Cammell Laird. Optimism and a gung-ho spirit seem to characterise the Sentinel Waggon Company at times, whereas Cammell Laird are businesslike and pragmatic. I have not yet been able to trace the next minute book (this one is in the care of Birmingham Libraries' Archive Service), but the extracts below trace an interesting period.

Some of the comments refer to standard gauge cars, and the LNER, as the largest customer, clearly wielded a lot of influence, but the narrow gauge cars followed the same line of development. I have reproduced the capital letter style of the book, but I cannot do justice to its beautiful handwriting. My own comments and summaries are in brackets.

Tuesday 16 November 1926
Mr Bailey (managing director) mentioned that the India Railway Board were becoming rather alarmed at the number of "Sentinel-Cammell" coaches recommended for purchase and had stated that there must be competition. (Sentinels must have "recommended" a very large number!)

This seemed hardly fair in view of the large amount of money spent by us in developing this vehicle, and Mr. Bailey stated that a letter would be written to this effect and sent to the proper quarter.

Mr. Boyd read a letter from Mr. H March, the Company's representative in China, stating that there was a possibility that we might be able to sell "Sentinel-Cammell" coaches on deferred payment terms to the Jardine Engineering Company for use on the Chinese Railways. The number mentioned was six Double Coaches and the period over which the payments would be spread two years.

After discussing the matter, the Committee agreed that there was undoubtedly a chance here of getting "Sentinel-Cammell" coaches into China, but that there was one unsatisfactory condition in the letter to the effect that if the Jardine Engineering Company had to wait for their money from the Railway Company, then we should have to do so also. While agreeing that we could allow payments by instalments with seven per cent interest over a period of two years, the Committee decided that we could not extend this period, and we should require some such terms as the following:- "Payment on shipment of twenty-five per cent of the capital sum, a second payment of twenty-five percent plus interest at the end of the first year, a third instalment at the end of eighteen months with a guarantee that the full amount would be paid at the end of two years."

Mr. Boyd promised to discuss this matter with the Sentinel Waggon Works Ltd.

Tuesday 14 December 1926

(Referring to LNER cars, the committee was told that) the question of the new direct drive to be fitted would not hold up delivery, having previously received Mr. Alley's (Sentinel MD) assurance to this effect.

Mr Boyd requested information as to the position in regard to the new design, and Mr Cockburn, who was asked to attend, stated that only the broad outline of the new drive had been worked out and that the details were far from being settled yet, so that the delivery of these coaches would in his opinion certainly be delayed. (The committee agreed that Mr. Alley should be told a chain-driven car would be acceptable in place of the expected new gear-driven model!)

Tuesday 18 January 1927

In regard to Sentinel-Cammell business, Mr. Bailey reported that the two coaches on order for the London and North Eastern Railway were to be supplied with chain drive, and that we were also to build a coach with the new gear drive which would, when completed, be placed at the disposal of the Railway Company and, it was expected, be purchased by them in due course.

Tuesday 15 March 1927

A statement of the result of our portion of the work on the "Sentinel-Cammell" Coach supplied to the North West Railway, Peru, was submitted and showed a profit of about 14 per cent on Actual Charges.

Mr. Bailey stated that owing to the development of the "Sentinel-Cammell" business, it was now necessary to afford more space for the erection of these vehicles. The Committee agreed that in the circumstances this was very necessary and confirmed the expenditure of £160, which was the amount required.

Tuesday 12 April 1927

(There was a report on the trial steaming of a new LNER gear-driven car – it had not been very satisfactory.) The Chairman then stated that Mr. Alley would no doubt give a full report of the trials at the forthcoming "Sentinel-Cammell" meeting.

(It was reported that LMS No. 1 was to be sold to the Jersey Eastern Railway who had also ordered another new one for £3,675.)

Tuesday 21 June 1927

(There was a discussion about the price being charged for the cars; losses had been sustained at first but now the price might be too high and so prejudice future orders in a growing business.)

Tuesday 12 July 1927

Referring to "Sentinel-Cammell" business, the Chairman stated that we were hoping to see a considerable improvement in the Partnership Accounts before the end of the year.

Mr. Good enquired regarding the progress of the gear-drive and the Chairman replied that satisfactory progress was being made. Before offering gear-drive, however, we were arranging to build one of this type for thorough testing.

Tuesday 13 September 1927

(The LNER thought that the company had been slow to deliver the new gear-driven coaches as they were still not available. They agreed to take 20 chain-driven cars on the understanding that a gear-driven coach would be ready for December. They would then order either 20 of these or 20 chain-driven, depending upon the result of trials. However, the Committee heard that there was no hope of promised delivery dates being met. They agreed to try as hard as possible and to discuss the problem with Mr. Alley.)

Tuesday 18 October 1927

(There had been a meeting with Mr. Alley and Mr. Gresley and the position was better) ...although our arrangement for engine and boiler for the gear-driven coach at present being built was similar to that adopted by Clayton Wagons Ltd., our representatives had been able to draw attention to various advantages which our design possessed.

Tuesday 15 November 1927

(The Sentinel-Cammell business was improving – the Chairman thought they were making too much profit! Prices were to come down.)

(Nottingham works had little business apart from erection of "Sentinel-Cammell" cars.)

15 May 1928

(At last the LNER gear-driven car was a success.)

Friday 20 July 1928

With regard to the "Sentinel-Cammell" Cars, it was reported that we had received from the "Sentinel" Company promises of delivery of their equipment for the various contracts on hand, so that we were now in a position to prepare a definite delivery programme. This programme would be produced at the next "Sentinel-Cammell" meeting.

Tuesday 18 September 1928

With regard to "Sentinel-Cammell" Cars, it was noted that we were being held up by delay in delivery of engines and boilers from Shrewsbury, and it was decided that more detailed information should be given in the report on deliveries promised to customers.

Tuesday 16 October 1928

(Prices had been put down, which)...would have the effect of bringing our estimates much more into line with the present cost of these Cars.

(LNER were to have cars delivered "two per week").

Mr Bailey stated that the amount of "Sentinel" work on hand was not as large as we had hoped, and the Chairman observed that possibly certain British Railway Officials were not so enthusiastic about these Cars as they might be.

It was mentioned that the Sentinel Company did not, when quoting against an enquiry, make a practice of consulting us as regards deliveries, and the Committee agreed that it would be well to draw their attention to this.

APPENDIX 3: TECHNICAL DETAILS

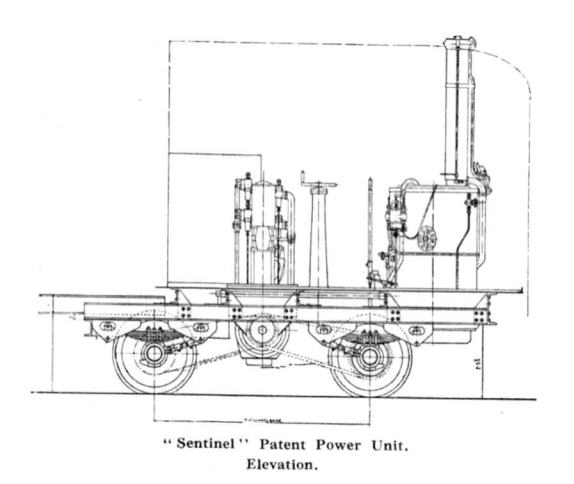

Early Cars

As the diagrams from the 1925 catalogue (left) show, the articulated narrow gauge cars had a simple arrangement of a forward boiler with vertical cylinders driving the wheels through two separate chains. According to the works list in Abbott, the first ten cars had horizontal cylinders but were otherwise similar (although the very first car *The Pioneer* No. 1, had only one chain, at least at first).

The diagram below, reproduced by Thomas and Thomas, seems to come from a lost (1926) catalogue, since it shows a horizontally-mounted engine with a crank-case. This is very similar to the arrangement shown in the 1927 locomotive catalogue which states that a variety of reduction gears can be provided and that final drive is by chain. Fourteen narrow-gauge cars were built with this arrangement. Clearly, in this as in the former system, the weight of the passenger car counterbalanced the weight of the boiler, though the inclusion of a water-tank in the horizontal diagram may indicate an attempt to further balance what must have been an unwieldy arrangement.

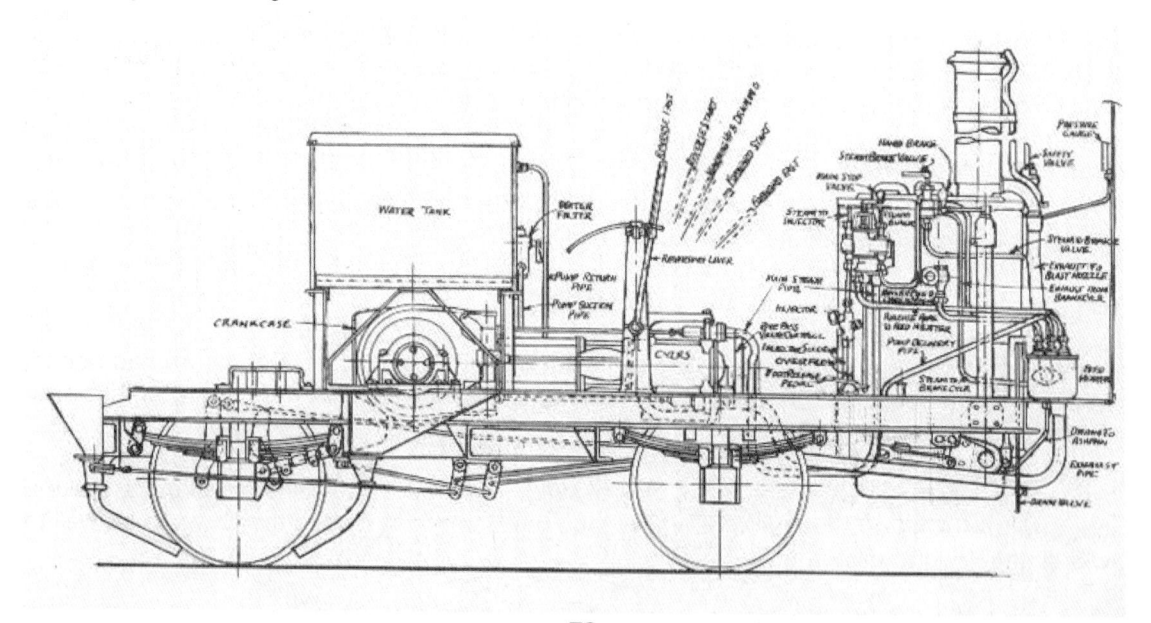

"Sentinel" Patent Power Unit. Elevation.

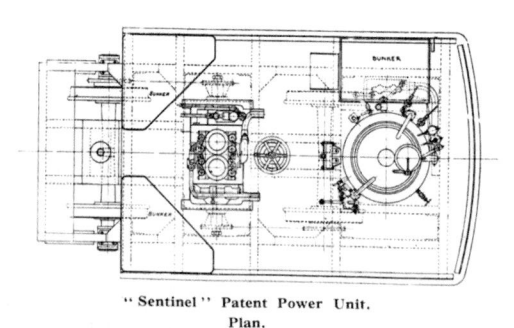

"Sentinel" Patent Power Unit. Plan.

Above: Sentinel patent power unit plan and elevation from 1925 catalogue. Below: diagram of articulated tractor.

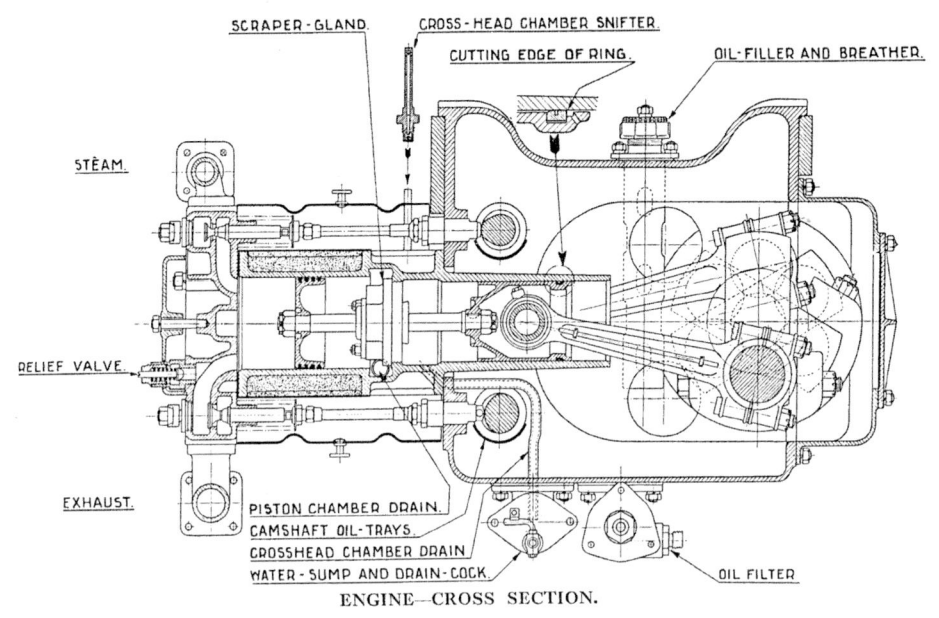

Cross section of rigid car engine

Rigid Cars

From 1928 a new six-cylinder single acting engine was introduced. This was horizontally mounted underfloor and drove through a cardan shaft.

The 1932 catalogue explains the working of the engine:

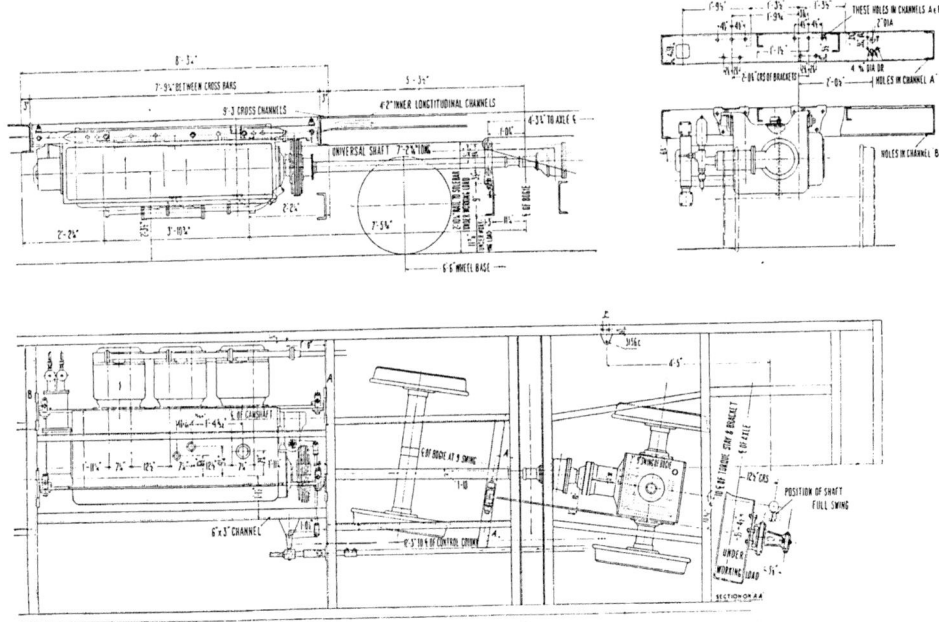

General arrangement of drive, rigid car, showing angle of movement of bogie

The 100-150 hp Engine is of the horizontal single-acting type, having six cylinders cast in pairs, 6 inch bore by 7 inch stroke, arranged for working with steam at 300 lbs. per square inch pressure and 650-750° F. temperature.

There is a lot about the quality of the castings and the maintenance-free nature of the engine in service. The drive is also explained in detail in the catalogue:

Drive is transmitted from the engine to a gearbox mounted on the driving axle by means of a Cardan Shaft of ample size. A large fabric disc joint at the engine end and a Universal Joint at the gearbox end provide for all angular movement. The shaft has a splined sliding joint at the joint end.

Boilers

When describing boilers, the 1922 (pre railcar production) catalogue contents itself with a picture and a description of the waggon boiler then in use. By the 1925 catalogue, however, when a good number of units had been manufactured, there is much more detail.

The Design is the outcome of experience with the working of over 5,000 of similar type. Although often operated by unskilled labour under adverse conditions, the results obtained have been entirely satisfactory. As will be seen from the illustration, the tubes are inclined, giving a rapid and natural circulation. Stoking is carried out through a Chute in the Boiler top. A Superheater Coil superheats the steam to approximately 600 F.

In the 1929 catalogue, five types of boiler are offered: there is the 100 hp (for "coal of reasonably good quality"), the 100 hp oil-fired, the 200 hp coal-fired, the 200 hp oil-fired and the "Bengal" boiler ("specially designed for the use of inferior coal such as is extensively used in India and other countries"). Three of these are vertical boilers, but the 200 hp are horizontal.

By the 1932 catalogue, the 200 hp boiler is referred to as the "Woolnough" and the "Bengal" boiler is described as the 100 hp and no reference is made to another boiler of that type. The reference to poor quality coal is, however, retained. (Someone must have been employed to continually update the catalogues, and that person seems to have been unwilling to discard previously written material!) In this catalogue, the oil-fired boiler for 100-150 hp rail cars is described, but there is no reference to oil-fired boilers for the 200 – 300 hp range.

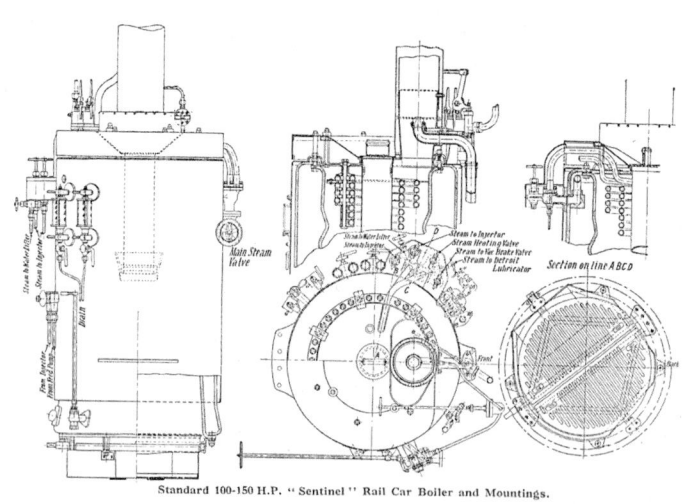

Standard 100-150hp boiler and mountings

Standard 100-150 H.P. "Sentinel" Rail Car Boiler and Mountings.

All the catalogues tell how wonderful the boilers are; one example, from 1932, must suffice:

As will be realised from this description and the illustrations, when the firebox is lowered out of the shell, every part of the water surface is not only accessible but is directly visible, so that scaling, re-tubing or re-expanding tubes are all extremely simple jobs which can usually be carried out within twenty-four hours.

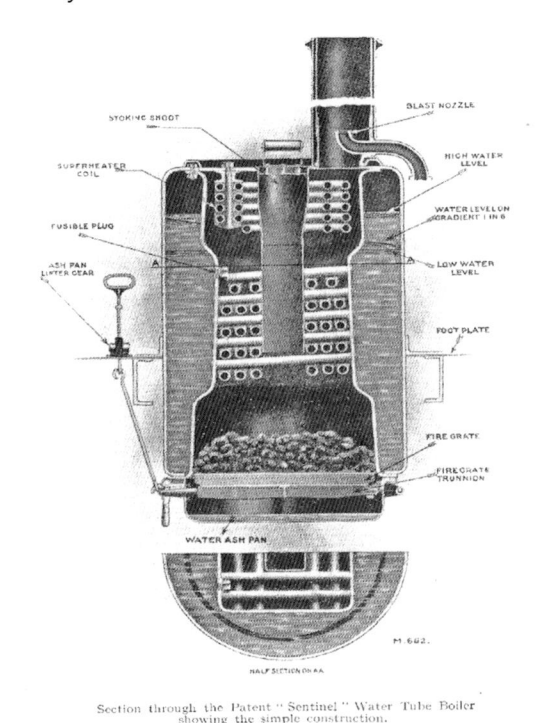

Section through the Patent "Sentinel" Water Tube Boiler showing the simple construction.

Sectional view of the "Sentinel" Patent Boiler.

Above left: section through patent Sentinel water tube boiler showing simple construction. Above right: sectional view of the Sentinel patent boiler. Below: engine in longitudinal section.

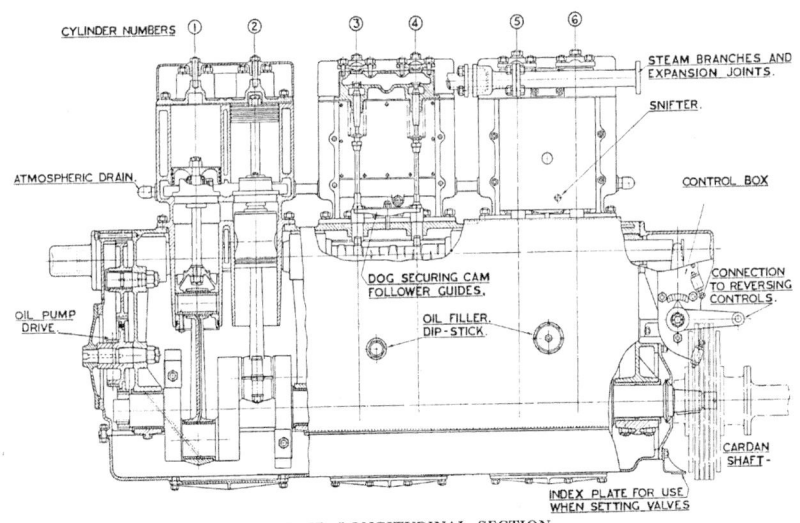

ENGINE—LONGITUDINAL SECTION.

75

APPENDIX 4 WORKS LIST

The works list turns up a number of problems which are, as yet unsolved. In particular, the dates of some works numbers appear to be out of sequence (or vice-versa) and there is a terrible gap in production between 1933 and 1937. Nevertheless, this is the best that can be produced at the moment.

Date	Works No	Cylinders	Gauge	Customer	Page No
6/1923	4863	2H	3'6"	Jersey Railways	12
7/1923	5155	2H	Metre	Orki Div, India	15
7/1923	5158	2H	Metre	Orki Div, India	15
1/1924	5159	2H	3'6"	Jersey Railways	12
8/1924	5234	2H	3'6"	Commonwealth Railways, Australia	15
11/1924	5245	2H	3'6"	Griffin Eng, South Africa	18
6/1925	5567	2H	3'6"	New Zealand Govt.	18
6/1925	5642	2H	3'6"	Newfoundland Govt Railway	20
6/1925	5711	2H	3'6"	Newfoundland Govt Railway	20
3/1925	5833	2H	3'6"	Jersey Railway	12
4/1926	6104	2V	2'6"	Bengal Nagpur (Satpura) Railway	22
4/1926	6126	2V	2'6"	Bengal Nagpur (Satpura) Railway	22
4/1926	6127	2V	2'6"	Bengal Nagpur (Satpura) Railway	22
1/1927	6289	2V	3'0"	North Western Railway, Peru	22
2/1927	6341	2V	2'6"	Barsi Light Railway	24
1927	6342	2V	2'6"	Barsi Light Railway	24
3/1927	6391	2V	2'6"	Ceylon Railway	25
1927	6392	2V	2'6"	Ceylon Government Railways	25
1927	6393	2V	2'6"	Ceylon Government Railway	25
6/1927	6462	2V	Metre	Iraq Railways	26
8/1927	6484	2V	3'0"	Salvador Railways	28
11/1927	6811	2V	Metre	Nizams State Railway	29
11/1927	6812	2V	Metre	Nizams State Railway	29
12/1927	6916	2V	3'6"	Gold Coast Railway	29
1928	7303	6H	2'6"	Ceylon Government Railways	25
1928	7304	6H	2'6"	Ceylon Government Railways	25
1928	7305	6H	2'6"	Ceylon Government Railways	25
1928	7314	6H	3'6"	Newfoundland Govt Railway	20
1928	7315	6H	3'6"	Newfoundland Govt Railway	20
1928	7316	6H	3'6"	Newfoundland Govt Railway	20
3/1928	7420	6H	Metre	Leopoldina Railway	30
3/1928	7434	6H	105cm	Palestine Railway	30
3/1928	7435	6H	105cm	Palestine Railway	30
1928	7564	6H	3'0"	Nor Oeste Railway Peru	22
7/1928	7584	6H	Metre	Bombay, Baroda & Central India Rly	36
1928	7585	6H	Metre	Bombay, Baroda & Central India Rly	36

1928	7586	6H	Metre	Bombay, Baroda & Central India Rly	36
8/1928	7606	6H	3'6"	Gold Coast Railway	29
1928	7607	6H	3'6"	Nigerian Railway	37
9/1928	7638	6H	Metre	Tanganyika Railway	38
1928	7639	6H	Metre	Tanganyika Railway	38
2/1929	7781	6H	Metre	Federated Malay States Railway	41
6/1929	7975	6H	3'6"	Gold Coast Railway	29
1929	7976	6H	3'6"	Gold Coast Railway	29
1929	8144	6H	3'6"	Nigerian Railways	37
1/1930	8189	6H	3'6"	Western Australia Government Railway	43
9/1930	8383	6H	3'6"	Den Spoorweg Maatschappij, Sumatra	44
4/1931	8410	6H	3'6"	Tasmanian Government Railway	44
1931	8411	6H	3'6"	Tasmanian Government Railway	44
2/1932	8470	6H	2'6"	NW State Rly, India, Kangra Valley Sec.	47
1932	8471	6H	2'6"	NW State Rly, India, Kangra Valley Sec.	47
1932	8472	6H	2'6"	NW State Rly, India, Kangra Valley Sec.	47
1/1932	8538	6H	Metre	Federated Malay States Railway	41
1932	8539	6H	Metre	Federated Malay States Railway	41
1932	8540	6H	Metre	Federated Malay States Railway	41
1932	8541	6H	Metre	Federated Malay States Railway	41
1932	8542	6H	Metre	Federated Malay States Railway	41
1931	8689	6H	3'6"	Nyasaland Railways	47
1931	8690	6H	3'6"	Nyasaland Railways	47
1933	8811	6H	3'6"	Tasmanian Government Railway	44
1933	8812	6H	3'6"	Tasmanian Government Railway	44
1933	8813	2x2H	Metre	Sao Paulo Railway, Brazil	51
1937	9201	6H	3'6"	Tasmanian Government Railway	44
1937	9202	6H	3'6"	Tasmanian Government Railway	44
1935	9232	6H	3'6"	Tanganyika Government Rly (see 9334)	38
1937	9234	6H	3'6"	Tasmanian Government Railway	44
1937	9235	6H	3'6"	Tasmanian Government Railway	44
1937	9238	6H	3'6"	Tasmanian Government Railway	44
1936	9265	6H	Metre	Leopoldina Railway, Brazil	29
1936	9266	6H	Metre	Leopoldina Railway, Brazil	29
1938	9267	6H	Metre	Federated Malay States Railway	41
1938	9268	6H	Metre	Federated Malay States Railway	41
1938	9269	6H	Metre	Federated Malay States Railway	41
1938	9295	6H	Metre	Federated Malay States Railway	41
1938	9296	6H	Metre	Federated Malay States Railway	41
1938	9297	6H	Metre	Federated Malay States Railway	41
1937	9334	6H	3'6"	Tanganyika Railway (mod of 9232)	38
1953	9553	6H	3'6"	Nigerian Railways	37
1953	9554	6H	3'6"	Nigerian Railways	37

ACKNOWLEDGEMENTS
(other than those given in the text)

Many references are made to "Abbott"; this is *Vertical Boiler Locomotives and Railmotors*, by Rowland A.S. Abbott published by The Oakwood Press 1989: ISBN 0 85361 385 0. After an appeal in *Narrow Gauge News* I was referred to this invaluable book by Bryant A. Hill of Oldham, who was so generous as to send me his copy. To him, my heartfelt thanks.

The Sentinel works list given in Abbott's book is undoubtedly often wrong, and many of the details included can only have been added later (running numbers which were used much later than the build date are given for some cars, for example). Nevertheless, Abbott remains an indispensable aid for the determined Sentinel spotter. I am indebted to Tony Thomas of the Sentinel Drivers' Club for much other information which helps unravel the works list. His book *The Sentinel* Vol. 2 is now out of print.

For Australian information I am indebted to many letters and notes from Darryl Grant.

Ray Ellis of Brisbane has added much to my knowledge of the Sentinel catalogues.

I am indebted to Antonio Augusto Gorni for much of the information about Brazilian matters.

Information about Jacks of Karachi was from S. Pai.

Thanks to Rabbi Dr. Walter Rothschild and Jeremy Topaz (Webmaster, HaRakevetmagazine.com) for information about Palestine Railways. Chen Melling of the Israel Railway Museum has been of inestimable help.

James Waite and Robin Patrick have given much help on the Sri Lankan cars.

Les Nixon contributed the memories of his Sentinel journey.

My sincere thanks go to Dr. Jeremy Howarth for his reading of the proofs.

Many others have helped; many are identified in the text and captions, but some just helped me along the way. Thanks to all.

BIBLIOGRAPHY

Books

The Jersey Railway by N.R.P. Bonsor, published by the Oakwood Press, 1962

The Sentinel: a history of Alley & MacLellan and The Sentinel Waggon Works. Volume 1. 1875-1930. by W.J.Hughes and Joseph L Thomas, published by David and Charles, 1973. Volume 2 of this history, by Thomas and Thomas, is referred to above.

Railways of the Channel Islands, by C. Judge, published by the Oakwood Press, 1992

Forced removal and the struggle for land and labour in South Africa: the Ngomane of Tenbosch, 1926–1954 by C Mather Department of Geography University of the Witwatersrand P.O. Wits 2050, Johannesburg, South Africa

Railways of the Andes by Brian Fawcett. Plateway Press 1963 (second edition 1997) ISBN 1 871980 31 3

Report on the State of road and railway competition and the possibilities of their future co-ordination and development, and cognate matters, in governors' provinces by K. G. Mitchell, A.C.G.I., MJnst.C.E., A.M.Inst.T, Road Engineer with the Government of India, AND L. H. Kirkness, MA, M.Inst.T., Officer on Special Duty with the Railway Board. (1933)

Railways of Sri Lanka, by David Hyatt, Comrac, London 2000. ISBN 0-9537304-0-9

Weak Foundations: The Economy of El Salvador in the Nineteenth Century by Héctor Lindo-Fuentes (University of California Press)

Permanent Way, Vol. II, The Story of the Tanganyika Railways by M. F. Hill: published 1957 by the East African Railways and Harbors, Nairobi, Kenya.

Steam Locomotives of East African Railways by R. Ramaer. A technical and historical outline of the motive power of both the British and German built lines. Published by David & Charles 1974, ISBN 0-7153-6437-5.

Malayan Railways, a brief introduction by Patrick Smith: B.O.R.H.T. 2006

Medan; A plantation city on the east coast of Sumatra 1870-1942 (Planters, the Sultan, Chinese and the Indian) by Dirk A. Buiskool

The Railways of Palestine and Israel by Paul Cotterell (Tourret Publishing 1984: ISBN 0-905878-04-3)

The Hedjaz Railway by R. Tourret (Tourret Publishing, 1989, ISBN 0-905878-05-1)

Indian locomotives, Part 3 – narrow gauge 1863 to 1940 by Hugh Hughes (Continental Railway Circle, 1994)

Make Straight the Way by Paul Cotterell ed. Chen Melling (Israel Railways, 2009, English edition ISBN 978-965-07-1795-7)

Magazine Articles

Australian Model Railway Magazine: various articles and December 2001 "The Sentinel Steam Rail Coach of the WAGR," (author unknown)

Australian Railway Historical Society Bulletin, February 1987: The Darwin Sentinel alias Leaping Lena, by Jim Harvey.

The New Zealand Model Rail Journal for October 1961, supplied by Robert Sweet, Treasurer - Glenbrook Vintage Railway

The New Zealand Railway Observer (NZ Railway and Locomotive Society), No. 165, autumn 1981: article by T.A. McGavin; and No 176, summer 1983-4: letter from J.A.T.Terry

The New Zealand Railways Magazine, Volume 2, Issue 5 (September 1, 1927): article by N. Blake.

Continental Railway Journal Autumn 1989 "Steam Railcars in Tanganyika," by R. Ramaer

Australian Railway Society Bulletin, February & March 1990, "Passenger Cars of the Tasmanian Government Railways," by H.J.W. Stokes.

Tasmanian Rail News No 233 "The Introduction of Corridor Passenger Trains on the TGR," by Andrew Dix

Websites

Industrial Locomotives of South Asia by Simon Darvill (http://www.ilsa.org.in/index.html)

Self-Propelled Cars on the Newfoundland Railway by David Page Branchline 2008 (http://www.railways.incanada.net/Circle_Articles/Article_Page03.html)

Newfoundland and Labrador Heritage: article by Robert Cuff http://www.heritage.nf.ca/society/railway_branch_lines.html

Wikipedia: various articles

http://community.livejournal.com/traveling_pics

Malcolm Wilton-Jones: http://searail.mymalaya.com/Classes/Sentinel.htm

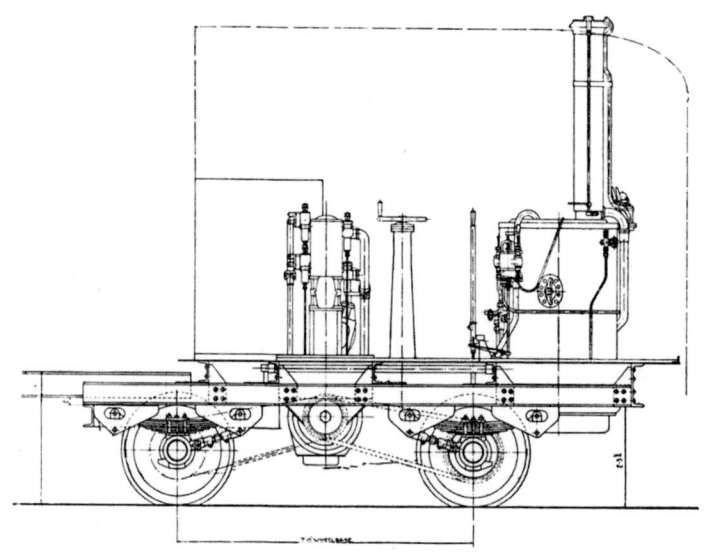

"Sentinel" Patent Power Unit.
Elevation.

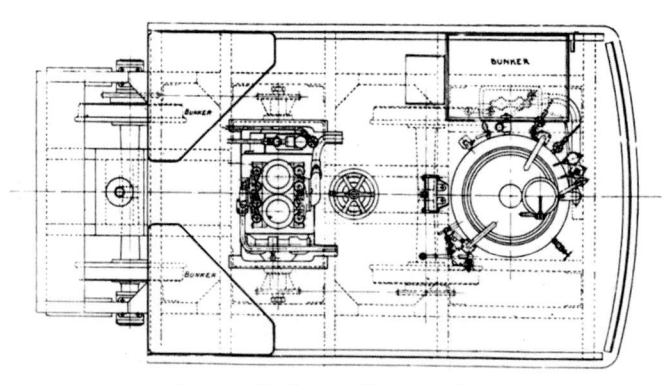

"Sentinel" Patent Power Unit.
Plan.

Sentinel patent power unit, plan and elevation

INDEX

Abbott 5
Adams & Co 17
Alley and MacLellan 3
Anthony R. Thomas 3
Articulated Cars 5,7,15,36
Barsi Light Railway 24
Bellarine Peninsula Railway 46
Bengal-Nagpur Railway 22
Boiler 74
Bombay, Baroda and Central India Railway (BB&CIR) 36, 57
Bonsor 12
Boyanup Railway Museum 43
Brazil 51
Brittany 14
Calthrop, E.R. 24
Cammell Laird & Co 5,69
Catalogue: 1922 4,5,61
Catalogue: 1925 62
Catalogue: 1927 66
Catalogue: 1929 67
Catalogue: 1931 68
Catalogue: 1932 11, 24, 28, 68
Ceylon Government Railways (CGR) 24, 25, 59
Chains 5
Commonwealth Rlys, Australia 15
Condensing apparatus 43
Controls 6, 67
Corridor connection 45
Cost 11
Cotterell, Paul 34
Cuff, Robert 20
Darvil, Simon 15
Deli Spoorweg Maatschappij (Deli Railroad Company) 44
Dematagoda 26
Diesel 29,30,32
Doble 14
Double-articulated 22
East African Railways and Harbours 40
Egyptian Railways 3
Ellis, Ray 48, 67
Fawcett, Brian 23
Federated Malay States (FMSR) 41
Gauge: 105cm 31
Gauge: 2'6" 15, 22, 24, 25, 47
Gauge: 3'0" 22, 28

Gauge: 3'6" 3, 18, 29, 43, 45, 47
Gauge: broad 22
Gauge: Cape 39
Gauge: metre 26, 29, 39, 42
Gauge: standard 3
Ghana *see Gold Coast*
Gold Coast Railway 29
Grant, Darryl 45
Great Western Railway 42
Gresley, Sir N 68
Griffin Engineering 18
Harvey, Jim 16
Hejaz railway 9,31
Horizontal cylinders 5, 15, 72
Hughes and Thomas 14
India 7
Injector 16
Inspection car 29
Iraq Railways 26
Israel Railway 31
(see also Palestine Railway)
Jack's of Karachi 15
Jersey Railway 5, 6,11,12, 52
Jersey Eastern Railway 14
Kangra Valley Railway 47
Kelani Valley Railway 25
Kent and East Sussex Railway 14
La Moye 14
Lavatory 20, 32, 34, 39, 43
Leaping Lena 16
Leopoldina Railway 29
Livery 5, 43, 46
Loading gauge 43
Locomotives 5
London Underground 8
London, Midland and Scottish Railway (LMS) 3,13
London, North-Eastern Railway (LNER) 3, 11, 16
Malawi 49
Malaya *see Federated Malay States*
Melling, Chen 34
Metropolitan Cammell *(and Metro-Cammell)* 5
Morrison, Allen 28
Natives 47
New Zealand Railways 8, 18, 54
Newfoundland Government Railway (NGR) 20, 56

Nigerian Railways 37
Nizam's State Railway 29
Normandy 14
North Australia Railway 15
North West Railway, Peru 22
North West State Railway, India 47
Nutty 5
Nyasaland Railways 47
Oil-burning 23, 46
Orki Division 15
Palestine Railway 8, 30
Peru *see North West State Railway*
Pioneer, The 12, 13, 15, 53
Portelet 13
Project Unigauge 24
Railway Gazette 26
Ramaer, R 38
Rigid cars 73
Rolls Royce 3
Saltley 69
Salvador Railways 28
Sao Paulo Railway, Brazil 51
Sentinel Drivers' Club 3
Sentul 42
Simpson and Bibby 4
Six horizontal cylinders 5, 20, 23, 26, 29, 37
Sleeping compartment 29
South Africa 18
Sri Lanka *see Ceylon*
Sumatra 43
Tanganyika Railway 38
Tanzania *see Tanganyika Railway*
Tasmanian Government Railway (TGR) 8, 43
Tasmanian Transport Museum 45
Thomas – *see Hughes and Thomas*
Tourret, R 9, 32
Transmission 18
Two-cylinder 18, 28, 72
Van Diemen Light Railway Soc 45
Vertical boiler 7
Vertical cylinders 7, 72
Waggons 4
Western Australian Government Railway (WAGR) 43
Williams, Kyrle. W 5
Woolnough Boiler 7

POSTSCRIPT

Whilst this book was in preparation, the author has been building his own Sentinel Railcar. To run on 7¼inch gauge, this car has been built to look like the early, Jersey, cars *The Pioneer* Nos. 1 & 2. It is not, in fact, a true Sentinel as its engine is a more conventional two-cylinder unit, built by Maxitrak of Staplehurst in Kent, but it is intended to remind observers of that short time in railway history when the steam railmotor was in the ascendant and Sentinels reigned supreme.

The 7¼in gauge *Sentinel No 7*, is designed to disassemble so that it can be easily transported in a saloon car, so it may well visit a railway near you.

The Sentinel No. 7 makes its debut at the Saffron Walden & District Society of Model Engineers' track at the Audley End Railway. March 15 2012 (David Nicholson)